The Joan Palevsky  Imprint in Classical Literature

In honor of beloved Virgil—

"O degli altri poeti onore e lume . . ."

—Dante, *Inferno*

The publisher gratefully acknowledges the generous contribution to this book provided by the Classical Literature Endowment Fund of the University of California Press Foundation, which is supported by a major gift from Joan Palevsky.

PERICLES

PERICLES

A SOURCEBOOK AND READER

STEPHEN V. TRACY

UNIVERSITY OF CALIFORNIA PRESS

Berkeley   Los Angeles   London

University of California Press, one of the most distinguished
university presses in the United States, enriches lives around the
world by advancing scholarship in the humanities, social sciences,
and natural sciences. Its activities are supported by the UC Press
Foundation and by philanthropic contributions from individuals
and institutions. For more information, visit www.ucpress.edu.

University of California Press
Berkeley and Los Angeles, California

University of California Press, Ltd.
London, England

Library of Congress Cataloging-in-Publication Data

Tracy, Stephen V., 1941–.
    Pericles : a sourcebook and reader / Stephen V. Tracy.
        p.   cm.
    Includes bibliographical references and index.
    ISBN 978–0-520–25603–3 (cloth, alk. paper)
    ISBN 978–0-520–25604–0 (pbk., alk. paper)
    1. Pericles, ca. 495–429 B.C.   2. Athens (Greece)—History.   3.
Statesmen—Greece—Athens—Biography.   4. Orators—
Greece—Athens—Biography.   I. Title.
DF228.P4T73   2009
938'.505092—dc22   2008034390
[B]

Manufactured in the United States of America

18   17   16   15   14   13   12   11   10   09
10   9   8   7   6   5   4   3   2   1

This book is printed on Cascades Enviro 100, a 100% post
consumer waste, recycled, de-inked fiber. FSC recycled certified
and processed chlorine free. It is acid free, Ecologo certified, and
manufactured by BioGas energy.

For Benjamin
and
Erik

CONTENTS

PASSAGES TRANSLATED

ILLUSTRATIONS

FIGURES

MAPS

ABBREVIATIONS AND PRIMARY SOURCES

In addition to explaining abbreviations used in this book, the following list includes, for students wishing to consult the original Greek sources, the Greek texts used or cited in the book. Greek texts of the authors listed are also available in the Loeb Classical Library series published by Harvard University Press. The Loeb editions provide the Greek text and an English translation on facing pages.

Aristophanes
> *Aristophanis Comoediae.* Edited by F. W. Hall and W. M. Geldart. Oxford, 1906.

[Aristotle] *Constitution of the Athenians*
> *Aristotelis Atheniensium Respublica.* Edited by F. G. Kenyon. Oxford, 1920.

Aristotle *Rhetoric*
> *Aristotelis Ars rhetorica.* Edited by W. D. Ross. Oxford, 1959.

FgrHist
> *Die Fragmente der griechischen Historiker.* Edited by F. Jacoby. Berlin and Leiden, 1923–.

Herodotus
> *Herodoti Historiae.* Edited by C. Hude. Oxford, 1927.

IG I³
> *Inscriptiones Graecae.* Vol. 1, *Inscriptiones Atticae anno Euclidis anteriores.* 3rd ed. Fasc. 1 edited by D. Lewis; fasc. 2 edited by D. Lewis and L. Jeffery. Berlin and New York, 1981 and 1994.

IG II²
> *Inscriptiones Graecae Euclidis anno posteriores.* Vols. 2–3. 2nd ed. Edited by J. Kirchner. Berlin, 1913–1931.

Isocrates
> *Isocrates.* 3 vols. Edited and translated by G. Norlin and L. van Hook. Loeb Classical Library. Cambridge, Mass., 1929–1945.

Lysias
> *Lysiae Orationes.* Edited by C. Hude. Oxford, 1912.

PCG
> *Poetae comici Graeci.* Edited by R. Kassel and C. Austin. Berlin and New York, 1983–.

Plato
> *Platonis Opera.* Edited by J. Burnet. Oxford, 1901–1907.

Plutarch
> *Plutarchi Vitae parallelae.* Vol. 1.2. Edited by K. Ziegler. Leipzig, 1964.

Sophocles
> *Sophoclis Fabulae.* Edited by H. Lloyd-Jones and N. G. Wilson. Oxford, 1992.

Thucydides
  Thucydidis Historiae. Edited by H. S. Jones. Oxford, 1942.
Xenophon
  Xenophontis Opera omnia. Edited by E. C. Marchant. Oxford, 1913.

PREFACE

This book about Pericles will fill, I hope, a need of teachers and students at high schools and colleges who are studying the golden age of Athens. That period is usually called the Periclean Age after Athens' greatest leader, Pericles. However, despite the undeniable importance of the man, there exists no book in English that collects in one place the scattered primary evidence about his life. Scholarly books on Pericles and his era, of course, appear with regularity in a variety of languages. Two recent works are W. Will, *Thukydides und Perikles* (Bonn, 2003), and A. Banfi, *Il governo della città: Pericle nel pensiero antico* (Bologna, 2003).

This modest sourcebook and reader has several purposes: to bring together in readable translations all of the passages pertaining to Pericles that were written by persons who either knew him personally or were in a position to know others who knew him well, to provide helpful interpretive comments on these passages, and to assess what Pericles' contemporaries may have thought of him.

This book is intended for students who have no knowledge of Greek and who also are likely to have very little knowledge of ancient Greece. Thus I have deliberately kept the notes and scholarly apparatus to a minimum, referring mainly to the primary sources. Basic information students will need to know I have tried to include in the text or in the glossary. The translations throughout are my own. My goal in translating is to be both accurate and clear. Strict accuracy occasionally has been sacrificed in favor of a turn of phrase that is understandable to contemporary students. In the case of the historian Thucydides, that most difficult of Greek stylists, I have out of necessity greatly simplified his complex sentence structure, but I have not tried to give him a false clarity. His meaning is at times opaque, and I have not disguised that fact in translating him.

The directors of the University of California Press some years ago paid me the compliment of inviting me to contribute this book. I trust this slim volume does not belie their confidence. I am indebted to the College of Humanities of the Ohio State University for the grant of a research leave for most of the 2000–2001 academic year, which enabled me to write an initial draft. Despite heavy administrative duties as Director of the American School of Classical Studies at Athens (2002–2007), duties that left little time for writing, I have now (five years later) finished the book. As I look back, my greatest debt is to my students, who over the last thirty years have shared their thoughts and questions with me. They are truly the coauthors of this volume. I also am indebted to the anonymous readers of the Press for detailed and helpful suggestions. Lastly, my wife, Professor June Allison, a fine Thucydidean scholar, and my son, Ben, now a senior in college—it is students his age and a bit younger for whom this book is primarily intended—have offered invaluable criticism of the manuscript in its various stages. For good or ill, however, I alone am responsible for what is on these pages.

> *The American School of Classical*
> *Studies / St. Augustine Beach*
> *Athens, Greece / St. Augustine, Florida*
> *December 2006 / August–September 2007*

Introduction

A BRIEF HISTORY OF ATHENS
IN THE FIFTH CENTURY

The century began with the Persian Wars when the Persians attacked Greece and Athens, first in 490 under Darius and then in 480/79 under his son Xerxes. There were memorable battles: Marathon in 490 where the Athenians soundly defeated the Persians; then in 480/79 Thermopylae, scene of the slaughter of the 300 Spartans by the Persians; Salamis, where in the straits between the island and the mainland the Athenian navy defeated the Persian fleet; and finally the Spartan-led victory over the land troops of Xerxes at Plataea (see map 1). These battles Herodotus recounted in epic fashion in his *Histories*. The Greeks were led in the fighting by the Spartans and the Athenians, who were allies at the time. At the end of the war the Spartans were the dominant force in the loosely formed Peloponnesian League but were content, in fact, to return home to Lacedaemon. The Athenians

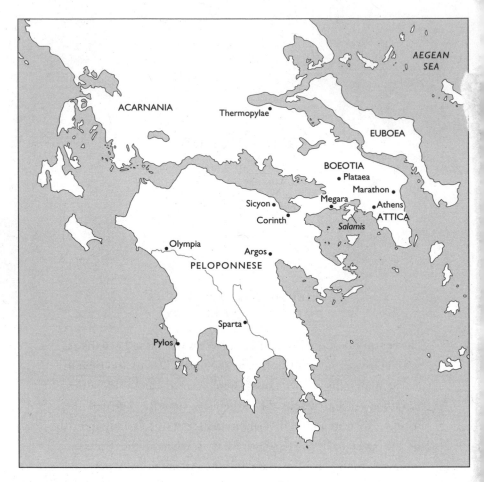

Map 1.   The Greek mainland

emerged from the war as a formidable naval power, a change largely conceived and put into place by the statesman and strategist Themistocles. The success of the Athenian triremes in the sea battle at Salamis against the large but cumbersome fleet of the Persians confirmed his strategy and, more important, allowed sailors and soldiers to play a significant role in the democracy at Athens. The century ended with the protracted war between the former allies that we refer to as the Peloponnesian War (431–404 B.C.), a war that the Spartans eventually won, ironically, with the aid of the Persians.

In the interim between these wars two interlocking phenomena made Athens a cultural and political power that would influence the rest of Western history: the creation of the Athenian empire and the development of the so-called golden age of Athens under Pericles. Following the defeat of Persia, the Greek city-states formed a defensive alliance, the Delian League, which the Athenians led and dominated almost from the beginning. This was probably inevitable because the Spartans, an infantry power, naturally had little interest in a naval league whose purpose was to keep the Persians out of the Aegean. League members contributed either ships or money, depending on their size and resources. The League had its center and treasury on Delos, the sacred island of Apollo, which was essentially the geographical hub among the participating cities (see map 2). Since the Athenians contributed the largest number of ships, they came to dictate policy to its membership. By midcentury they had turned the League into their empire. In 454 the Athenians transferred the treasury from Delos to Athens, allowing them to control expenditures as well as the collection of monies. The payments had by this time become tribute exacted from subject states, not con-

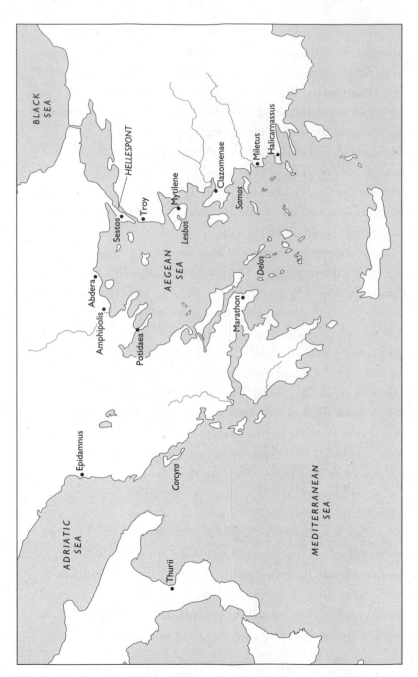

Map 2. Greece, the Adriatic, and the Aegean

tributions from free allies. Defections from the new empire were not tolerated. The revolts of larger islands like Thasos in the mid-460s and Samos in the 440s were put down harshly. Allies that revolted were brought back into the fold and heavily fined in the form of increases in their annual tribute. Thasos, for example, had its payment increased from 3 to 27 talents, an enormous sum.

At the same time that the Delian League was developing into the Athenian empire "radical democracy" was beginning to emerge in Athens. Ordinary people, augmented by the newly empowered sailors, took greater control of the political direction of the city from the old landed aristocrats. Leaders of the people, among them Ephialtes and Pericles, introduced measures that resulted by midcentury in a thoroughgoing direct democracy. The vibrant self-confidence that came from the defeat of the Persians, coupled with peace in the Aegean and income from the empire, contributed to a tremendous blossoming of Athenian culture that matched its military expansion. The grand building program on the Acropolis is one of the symbols of this period of growth and enlightenment, even if money from the subject allies sponsored the construction. One of the themes of the Parthenon sculptures (447–432 B.C.) was civilization's victory over barbarism: Olympian gods over the giants, Greeks over Trojans, humans over the half-man, half-beast centaurs. The superiority of Athens and the Athenians was another theme. Indeed, the building itself served as a very visible manifestation of Athens' might. This message of Athenian pride could only incur jealousy and antagonize other Greeks.

Sparta and its allies in the Peloponnese, particularly Corinth, clearly felt threatened by the expansion of Athenian power and influence and in the late 460s initiated campaigns designed to limit it. The tension stemmed primarily from Athenian alliances with former allies of Sparta, namely, Megara and Argos (see map 1). In addition Athens won and lost Boeotian cities north of Attica. Historians identify these scattered armed responses collectively as the First Peloponnesian War. These conflicts failed to solve long-term animosities; rather, they aggravated jealousies and territorial disputes. The Athenians, with the aid of their allies and under the leadership of Pericles' rival, Cimon, succeeded in pushing the Persians from the sea at the battle of the Eurymedon on the southern coast of Asia Minor in 468(?) only to suffer a miserable defeat in 454 in Egypt, where they had gone to support an uprising against Persia. Nonetheless, in 445, encouraged by Pericles, the Athenians and Spartans agreed to the Thirty Years' Peace.

In the late 430s, however, they came into direct conflict with one another, almost without actively pursuing it, and primarily through the agency of the Corinthians. The Athenians were convinced by the inhabitants of Corcyra (present-day Corfu), a colony of Corinth, to aid them in dealing with their own colony of Epidamnus (see map 2). Corinth, the most influential of Sparta's allies, appealed to the Spartans to thwart an Athenian alliance with Corcyra, which was after all, the Corinthians argued, their colony. The subsequent conflict in the west around Corcyra was the flashpoint that started the Peloponnesian War; but, according to Thucydides (1.23.6), the real reason for the war was a general fear of Athenian aggression and power.

This war was a classic struggle between two powerful rival cities. Sparta boasted the best infantry, and Athens the greatest navy of the time. The Athenians had a vibrant economy that flourished primarily because of their democratic system of government and the resources of their empire, while the Spartans had an oligarchic system, ruled by two kings, and prided themselves on four hundred years of constitutional stability. Contrary to expectation, even that of Thucydides himself, the democratically run, culturally superior Athens did not win the war but was essentially starved into submission in 404 when Sparta was able to blockade the harbor (the Piraeus) of its seafaring rival.

The twenty-seven-year war can be considered in phases. The first is the ten-year period called the Archidamian War, named after the Spartan king whose strategy it was to invade Attica annually, destroying crops and homes. Pericles' response was to harass the shores of the Peloponnese with the fleet. He rightly saw that it would have been disastrous to try to engage the superior infantry of the Spartans on land. These opening conflicts and the Periclean strategy were disrupted by the outbreak of the plague in 430. The plague killed off perhaps a third of the population in Athens, many of whom had streamed into the city to avoid the Spartan incursions. Although Pericles failed to be reelected general the next year, he was soon forgiven by the majority and reinstated. But in that year, 429, Pericles himself died of the plague.

The Athenians held to Pericles' strategy, and through the agency of the generals Demosthenes and Cleon were able to defeat a large Spartan force in Pylos and capture a significant number of pure-blooded Spartiates. This loss contributed not a little to the Spartan willingness to agree to a peace in 421 authored by the Athenian general Nicias.

This peace Thucydides claims was no peace at all, because some major players, notably the Corinthians, refused to sign. But it gave the Athenians the opportunity to launch a massive expedition against Sicily (415–413 B.C.), particularly against Syracuse. Athens had always had an interest in the West, especially since Sicily provided much of Sparta's grain, but the doomed expedition was also fueled by imperialistic dreams. The Athenians staked much of their naval resources on the venture. The outcome was a disaster caused in large measure, according to Thucydides, by the Athenians themselves, who removed the one man who might have carried it off, Pericles' nephew, the energetic and flamboyant Alcibiades. Furthermore, the Spartans, again encouraged by the Corinthians and now by the exiled Alcibiades, had reopened the war in the east by moving into the Aegean.

The last phase of the war had begun. Although their naval superiority had been severely damaged by the Sicilian disaster, the Athenians with their characteristic energy put together a new fleet for service in the Aegean. The Spartans encouraged major Athenian allies to defect and solicited the aid of Persia in support of their naval efforts primarily by acquiring money to develop their fleet of warships. A series of defections of the bigger islands, coupled with the collapse of the democracy in Athens in 411, seemed to spell the end, but the restoration of the democracy and the return of Alcibiades from exile enabled the Athenians to carry on. Finally, two defeats at sea and political turmoil at home paved the way for Athens' final capitulation, which was secured by the Spartans' blockade of the Piraeus. The blockade ended the naval empire of Athens both symbolically and actually.

CHRONOLOGY

The following list provides dates important for the history of Athens in this period and for the life of Pericles.

		ca. 495	Birth of Pericles to Xanthippus and Agariste
490	Battle of Marathon		
483	Silver vein found at Laurion, used to build fleet		
480	Battle of Salamis		
479	Battle of Plataea		
	Xanthippus takes Sestos and executes Persian governor and his son		
478/7	Founding of Delian League		
472/1	Ostracism of Themistocles	472	Pericles produces Aeschylus's *Persians*
468?	Battle of the Eurymedon (defeat of Persians)		
465–63	Revolt of Thasos	463	Pericles prosecutes his rival Cimon
		462/1	Reforms of Ephialtes
		461	Ostracism of Cimon

ca. 460   Birth of Thucydides

460–447 "First Peloponnesian War"

457   Athenians take over
               Megara, Aegina

454   Athenian defeat   454   Pericles leads
               in Egypt   expedition against
                                                     Sicyon, Acarnania
               Treasury of Delian
               League moved to
               Athens

452   Five Years' Truce
               between Athens and
               Peloponnesians

                                      451   Citizenship Law
                                                     of Pericles

450 or
449 (?)   Peace with Persia
               (Peace of Callias)

447–432 Construction of Parthenon

                                      447/6   Pericles subdues
                                                     Euboea

445   Thirty Years' Peace
               between Athens and
               Sparta

444/3	Founding of Thurii		
		443	Ostracism of Thucydides son of Melesias
440	Revolt of Samos	ca. 440	Pericles the Younger born
438	Gold and ivory statue of Athena by Phidias dedicated in the Parthenon		
437	Work begins on Propylaea		
435–432	Corcyra in conflict with Corinth; Athens becomes ally of Corcyra		
432	Work on Propylaea interrupted	432	Pericles defends Megarian decree

431–404 Peloponnesian War

| 431 | First invasion of Attica by Spartans | 431 (November?) | Pericles' funeral oration |

430 (spring– summer)		430 Pericles leads raids on northeast coast of Peloponnese
Second invasion of Attica by Spartans		
Plague breaks out in Attica		Pericles' sons Xanthippus and Paralus die
		Pericles charged, fined, and removed from office
		429 (spring)
		Pericles reelected general
		429 (late summer or early fall)
		Death of Pericles from plague
424	Thucydides exiled for twenty years	
421	Peace of Nicias	
416	Melian Dialogue	

THE LIFE OF PERICLES

Almost all great men quickly become figures of legend; they take on larger-than-life dimensions. Perhaps, with the single exception of Alexander the Great, this is true of Pericles more than any other historical figure of antiquity. He was a giant among giants and gave his name to one of the most brilliantly creative times in the history of the world. We call this period the Periclean Age, yet it was an era—and Athens was a city—that produced a host of astonishing talents. Sophocles, Euripides, and Socrates were among Pericles' contemporaries. However, although we speak of the Socratic method, we do not speak of the age of Socrates. And although there were other outstanding political leaders in Athens, such as Cimon, the son of Miltiades, still it is Pericles who stood out for his contemporaries and for posterity.

A man of contradictions, Pericles came from old aristocratic stock but became the champion of the people, the acknowledged leader of the democracy. He promulgated a law limiting citizenship to those whose mothers and fathers were both Athenian but himself had a longtime relationship with Aspasia, a foreign woman from Miletus with whom he had a son. The comic poets caricature Pericles as Zeus-like in his aloofness, yet the people elected him repeatedly to be their general. Clearly they trusted him and, just as clearly, had grounds to do so.

Reliable facts about Pericles, the son of Xanthippus, of the district Cholargus are few. He was born by about 495 B.C. His mother, Agariste, hailed from an important aristocratic family from Sicyon (Herodotus 6.131; see below, p. 11). Her uncle— her father's brother—was Cleisthenes, the reputed founder of Athenian democracy. Pericles' earliest public acts reveal that he was a supporter of the Athenian statesman Themistocles, the architect of the victory at Salamis.

Themistocles had built up the Athenian navy in the years after Darius's attack on Athens at Marathon in 490. He relied on the ordinary people who manned and maintained the fleet; these were not the landed aristocrats, but rowers, dockworkers, and others who made a living from or on the sea. Themistocles was probably the first real leader of the *demos,* the ordinary people. Thus it seems notable that Pericles took on the financial responsibility for producing Aeschylus's play *The Persians* in the spring of 472 (*IG* II² 2318 line 10). This drama celebrated the great Athenian naval victory over the Persians eight years earlier at Salamis. It explicitly reminded the Athenians of the great debt they owed to those who manned the fleet and in particular to the Athenian most responsible for the victory, Themistocles. The drama taps intense feelings of patriotism, and Pericles' backing of the play probably marked his emergence as a politician in his own right.

Pericles unsuccessfully prosecuted his rival Cimon in 463 on a charge of malfeasance in handling the siege of Thasos. He joined in the late 460s with another radical leader named Ephialtes to assume leadership of the people. Ephialtes spearheaded an attack on the Council of the Areopagus, one of the bastions of aristocratic power, and reduced it from an influential policy-making body to a law court that tried homicide cases. Pericles and Ephialtes also tried to open up the organs of government to ordinary citizens. At the time, these were radical measures that created a lot of animosity. Ephialtes was assassinated, leaving Pericles as the primary leader of the people.

For an entire generation, that is, for almost thirty years, Pericles was both leader of the people and a member of the board of ten generals. He had some strong opponents, such as Cimon son of Miltiades, who opposed his anti-Spartan policies, and Thucydides son of Melesias, who opposed his public-building program. Cimon was ostracized early in 461, and, with Pericles lending his help, Thucydides was forced into exile in 444 or 443. Pericles introduced various important measures, including pay for jurors[1] and the restriction of citizenship to those whose parents were both Athenian citizens.[2] The first measure enabled even the most humble citizens to participate as jurors; the second apparently sought to address the uncontrolled growth in the citizen rolls in the thirty years since the Persian Wars. Considerations of self-identity and self-interest may also have influenced the Athenians to pass the second measure as a means of ensuring that those who benefited from the privileges of citizenship were legitimately entitled to do so.

Through his position as general, Pericles must have built up a very strong power base. Among his friends and associates were, it seems, Protagoras[3] and Anaxagoras,[4] the sophists, and Phidias, the sculptor.[5] By 450 Pericles was certainly recognized by all as the most powerful person in Athens, and the leader of the city. He and his associates were not, however, immune from

---

1. Aristotle *Politics* 1274a7–8; Plato *Gorgias* 515e5–7.

2. *Constitution of the Athenians* 26.4; C. Patterson, *Pericles' Citizenship Law of 451–50 BC* (Salem, Mass., 1981).

3. For Protagoras, see below, pp. 116–18.

4. Isocrates *Antidosis* 235; Plato *Phaedrus* 269–270 (below, p. 135), *Alcibiades* I 118c.

5. Aristophanes *Peace* 600 ff. (below, p. 101).

attack. His lady friend, Aspasia, and Anaxagoras were probably dragged into court.[6] Phidias was accused of stealing and went to Olympia (see map 1) to work. Pericles too was apparently accused of misappropriating funds.

Pericles was an advocate of Athenian power, particularly Athens' naval power, and spent most of his life expanding and protecting Athens' influence on the mainland and in the Aegean. He seems to have inherited this focus from his father, Xanthippus, who was a general in the Persian Wars and who, at the conclusion of the wars, according to Herodotus (9.114–121), successfully besieged Sestos, the main city on the European side of the Hellespont (see map 2), and drove out the Persians. Surely his goal was to establish, even briefly, an Athenian presence on this crucial grain route from the Black Sea region. In doing this, Xanthippus was one of the first proponents of what became the Athenian empire. There can be little doubt that these activities of his father exercised a strong influence on Pericles.

We can surmise from his election as general year after year for some twenty-five years that Pericles was an extremely successful leader on campaigns and in combat. The ancient Athenians had little tolerance for generals who lost battles. They were recalled, demoted, exiled, or executed. For example, Thucydides, the historian, and a general during the Peloponnesian War, failed to save Amphipolis for the Athenians in 424 and was exiled for twenty years, as he himself tells us (5.26.5). Not only was Pericles successful, but he must also have had lady luck on his side at times. We really know nothing of him as a military leader, however, having no firsthand accounts, as we do for Julius Caesar, for

6. Plutarch *Pericles* 32.

example, of his comportment on the battlefield. It is certain, however, that his position as general gave him high prominence among his contemporaries.

We know the bare facts of his campaigns, primarily from Thucydides. In the mid-450s as one of the board of ten generals elected by the Athenian people, Pericles led a campaign in the Gulf of Corinth against Sicyon (see map 1), his mother's ancestral city, on the southern side of the gulf and then into Acarnania at its northwestern end (Thucydides 1.111.2–3). In 446 he led the forces that crossed to the island of Euboea to put down a revolt, but returned with them to deal with a Spartan invasion of Attica. Having eliminated that threat, he went back to Euboea, which he brought to heel (Thucydides 1.114).[7] He also served as general during 440 and 439, putting down the revolt of the powerful island ally Samos (Thucydides 1.116–117).[8] Though his name never appears on the inscribed building accounts that survive, Pericles certainly played a significant role in the great building program on the Acropolis that began in the early 440s and continued until the outbreak of the Peloponnesian War in 431. The chief ornament of that program was the Parthenon, which was constructed between 447 and 432 B.C.

7. The rumor was that Pericles dealt with the Spartans by using public funds to bribe King Pleistoanax to withdraw. When asked what he had expended the money for, he replied, "For what was necessary." This is reported by Plutarch (*Pericles* 23.1) and vouched for by Thucydides (2.21.1, 5.16.3) and Aristophanes (*Clouds* 859; below, p. 29).

8. Plutarch *Pericles* 20 is the sole source for Pericles' leadership of an expedition to the Black Sea region during the early 430s. *IG* I³ 1180, an extremely fragmentary casualty list, has been ascribed by some to this campaign. It is possible but hardly certain.

He also, it appears, realized that armed conflict with the Spartans and their allies was bound to happen, and carefully prepared his city for the conflict. It was his strategy, and he maintained it steadfastly, to move the citizenry within the walls of the city and not to engage the superior Spartan army on land, but to send the Athenian fleet around the Peloponnese to harass Spartan towns. Thus the Athenians were cooped up in the city when the plague hit in 430. Demoralized by their sufferings, the people blamed Pericles and removed him from the generalship but soon reelected him (Thucydides 2.60–65.4). Pericles himself caught the plague and died from it during late summer or early autumn of 429. Many, both ancient and modern, feel that had he not died of the plague at the beginning of the war he might well have led his city to victory. In any case, his untimely death, as tragic as it was, helped catapult him to legendary status.

Pericles had two sons, Paralus and Xanthippus, by his wife, whose name we do not even know. Both sons died before their father during the plague. After divorcing his wife, Pericles formed a lasting relationship with Aspasia, with whom he had a son, Pericles the Younger.[9] Pericles also assumed guardianship over Alcibiades, whose father, Cleinias, was killed in battle in 446.[10] We do not know the exact relationship between Pericles and his ward, except that they were related by blood. Other immediate family members included a sister (whose name has not come down to us), who also died during the plague, and a slightly older brother named Ariphron, a shadowy figure who

9. On Aspasia, see below, p. 97.
10. Isocrates *On the Chariots* 28.

was known only from a passing mention in the writings of the philospher Plato until 1991, when three ostraca cast against Ariphron were reported from the German excavations in the main cemetery of Athens, the Ceramicus.[11] The ostraca appear to date to about 470. That Ariphron was a target for ostracism at this time suggests that rivals initially expected that he, the older son, and not Pericles, would be Xanthippus's political successor.[12]

The foregoing is about all that we know reliably concerning the life of this most famous Athenian leader. The reason for this lamentable fact is that our sources are largely lacking; we have, for example, no biography of Pericles until Plutarch. Indeed, Plutarch's *Life* appears to have been the first real biography of Pericles ever written. Plutarch, however, lived more than five hundred years after Pericles; his biography is anecdotal and of questionable reliability.[13] Furthermore, the greatest part of Pericles' political activity fell between the end of the Persian Wars in 479 and the beginning of the Peloponnesian War in 431. The two great historians of the age, Herodotus and Thucydides, each wrote accounts of the respective wars but did not deal with the interim period except, in the case of the latter, very briefly. In the first book of his *History of the Peloponnesian War* Thucydides included an overview of the intervening period known as the *pentecontaetia*, the "fifty-year interval" (1.89–118.2).

11. D. M. Lewis, "Megakles and Eretria," *Zeitschrift für Papyrologie und Epigraphik* 96 (1993): 51.

12. See the chapter on the archaeological evidence for the whole matter of ostracism and known ostraca cast against Pericles.

13. See below, pp. 145–49.

Thus we have no account from an ancient historian of Pericles' political activity for the greater part of his life. Thucydides, however, does give us a portrait of Pericles in the last three years of his life, a valuable picture that deserves careful study. In addition, we know that Ion of Chios (*FgrHist* 392) and Stesimbrotus of Thasos (*FgrHist* 107) each wrote a sketch of Pericles. These works do not survive, however, and it is difficult to get a sense of them. Stesimbrotus's pamphlets recounted the lives of Themistocles, Thucydides (the politician, *not* the historian), and Pericles; his purpose seems to have been to depict these Athenian leaders in negative terms.[14] Ion recorded visits that he had with distinguished persons, among them Pericles.

Writing about 330 B.C., that is, a century after Pericles died, Aristotle, or a member of his school, gave a very sketchy history of Athens in the work entitled *The Constitution of the Athenians,* which includes the following comments on Pericles:

> In the archonship of Antidotus (451/0) on account of the large number of citizens it was passed on the motion of Pericles that no one should share in the city who was not born from citizen parents. After this Pericles came to the fore as a popular leader and gained a reputation for the first time when as a young man he brought suit against the general Cimon over his accounts. As a result the government became more democratic. He removed some of the powers of the Areopagus and particularly turned the city toward naval power. In consequence, the people took courage and appropriated the entire government more to themselves. Forty-eight years after the battle of Salamis in the archonship of Pythodorus (432/1) the war against the

14. On Stesimbrotus's slander of Pericles, see below, p. 105, n. 9.

Peloponnesians broke out. The people were shut up in the city and became accustomed to earn money by military service. Partly on purpose and partly from circumstance they took over running the government themselves. Pericles instituted pay for jury duty. . . . (26.4–27.3)

While Pericles was in charge of the people, the affairs of government were quite good; when he died, they became worse. Then people for the first time accepted as leader a man not approved by the better class. Before this the better class always held the offices and led the people. In the beginning the first leader of the people was Solon, second was Peisistratus, both wellborn and of known families. When the tyranny was dissolved, there was Cleisthenes, of the Alcmeonid clan, and he had no opposition when Isagoras and his followers fell. After this, Xanthippus led the people and Miltiades the aristocrats, next Themistocles the one group and Aristeides the other. Following these, Ephialtes led the democrats and Cimon, the son of Miltiades, the wealthy. Next Pericles the democrats and Thucydides, the relative of Cimon [not the historian], the others. When Pericles died, Nicias who died in Sicily led the upper classes, while Cleon, the son of Cleaenetus, led the people. He more than anyone seems to have corrupted the people with his uncontrolled impulses. (28.1–3)

This is largely an academic piece that is concerned to give a logical account in a very brief compass. Class distinctions, particularly an aristocratic bias, openly slant the presentation. The careful balance in the second paragraph between leaders of the aristocrats on the one side and leaders of the people on the other is surely false and covers up a political complexity that we can never recover. Pericles' father, Xanthippus, and Miltiades, for example, never led opposing factions. The first section provides three important facts, that Pericles carried through a law about citizenship in 451/0, that he prosecuted Cimon, and that he introduced pay for jury duty. Otherwise, the account is very general and schematic in describing the increasing power of the people and the decay in leadership after Pericles' demise.

This in broad outline is the sketchy picture we can piece together of Pericles. With the advantage of distance we can see clearly his importance and indeed the brilliance of his policies. His building program for Athens not only beautified the city but also created jobs and advertised Athens' might. He not only assumed the leadership of the people but also at the same time increased his own power base by providing pay to many average citizens, pay that enabled many of them, probably for the first time, to participate in the system. His consistent efforts to strengthen the empire built up Athenian power, particularly the power of the fleet. This in turn led to his naval strategy for dealing with the Spartan challenge to Athenian dominance.

While posterity for the most part has praised Pericles as a statesman,[15] strident critics in his own day attacked every one

---

15. Admiration of Pericles and of the democracy at Athens has not, of course, been unanimous. The hostile tradition that treats Pericles as a crass demagogue began with his contemporaries; it was adopted by no less a figure than Alexander Hamilton, who in *The Federalist Papers* no. 6 singles out Pericles as a leader who for personal reasons "was the primitive author of that famous and fatal war," namely, the Peloponnesian War. See also the interesting book of J. Tolbert Roberts, *Athens on Trial: The Anti-democratic Tradition in Western Thought* (Princeton, 1994); she traces the sometimes virulent indictments of Athenian democracy from its creation to the time of the American and French revolutions.

of his policies.[16] Bringing together all the surviving contemporary or near-contemporary evidence about him may offer a clearer understanding of the achievements of this greatest of all ancient statesmen and a stronger sense of his qualities as a human being.

16. The parallels with Abraham Lincoln are many—a decisive leader in a terrible and unpopular war, now revered as the great emancipator, but in his own day heatedly opposed and at times subjected to slanderous personal attacks. For a recent study, see Doris Kearns Goodwin, *Team of Rivals: The Political Genius of Abraham Lincoln* (New York, 2005)

The Primary Sources

Pericles' Writings

No written work by Pericles has come down to us and, except for some speeches that he may have committed to writing and measures that he sponsored in the Council and the Assembly, we have no sure knowledge that Pericles himself wrote any-thing.[1] This loss of his direct words is a great pity, for contemporary and near-contemporary sources—namely, Thucydides, the comic poets, and Plato—describe him as the greatest orator of his time.[2] Eupolis in his comedy the *Demes,* which survives

1. At least some decrees attributed to Pericles survived in Plutarch's day (*Pericles* 8.7); in the 50s B.C. the Roman politician Cicero had seen purported speeches of Pericles (*De oratore* 2.93, *Brutus* 27). They were probably not gen-uine and are dismissed as composed by others by the Roman authority on rhetoric, Quintilian, about 75 A.D. (3.1.12, 12.2.22, 12.10.49).

2. Thucydides describes him as "first among the Athenians at that time and the man most effective in speech" (1.139.4; see below, p. 52); Plato styles him "the most perfect of all in rhetorical skill" (*Phaedrus* 269e).

only in fragments, includes the following exchange about Pericles, a high compliment indeed (*PCG* V 102):

> A) That man was the most powerful speaker of all.
> Whenever he came forward, like a great sprinter
> coming from ten feet behind, he bested his rivals.

> B) You say he was fast . . . A) But, in addition to his speed,
> persuasion somehow or other sat on his lips,
> so entrancing was he. He alone of the politicians
> customarily left his sting in his hearers.

Thucydides, who was perhaps in his midtwenties or older at the outbreak of the Peloponnesian War, had the opportunity to hear Pericles speak, one would assume, on a number of occasions. Whether he actually did or not, we have no way of knowing. He does not volunteer such information. In any case, Thucydides puts three speeches in Pericles' mouth in the first two books of his *History*.[3] Magnificent though they are, these are compositions by Thucydides, not the precise words of Pericles. Indeed, Thucydides admits in his *History* that it was difficult for him and his informers to remember the exact words spoken in the speeches on each occasion (1.22.1); but he adds that he composed them "adhering as closely as possible to the overall spirit of what was actually said." He also says in this same passage that he has recounted "what he thought each speaker needed to say in a given situation."

Apart from these speeches of Pericles recorded in Thucydides, we possess nearly a dozen turns of phrase that appear to

---

3. 1.140–144, 2.35–46 and 60–64. These speeches are translated and discussed below.

be either actual quotes or close paraphrases of Pericles. These are isolated passages for which we do not in most cases have an adequate context. When questioned about a politically sensitive expenditure during an annual audit of his official accounts in 446, Pericles replied with firm brevity that he had spent it "for what was necessary."[4] The temerity of this response sufficiently captured the imagination of his fellow Athenians that Aristophanes, more than twenty years later, could have old Strepsiades quote it in an absurd context in the *Clouds* (858–859). When questioned by his son about his slippers, the old man retorts, "Like Pericles, I lost them 'for what was necessary.' "[5]

Aristotle in his *Rhetoric* cites Pericles for his use of two striking similes and two arresting metaphors. In the funeral speech he gave probably in 439 over the dead in the Samian War, Pericles said that "the youth who had perished in the war had vanished from the city just as if someone had removed the spring from the year" (1411a2–4; cf. also 1365a31–33). Near the beginning of the Peloponnesian War he exhorted his fellow citizens "to remove Aegina, the sty in the eye of Piraeus" (1411a15–16). He likened the Samians "to kids who get bread but go on crying" and the Boeotians, "since they continuously fight with each other, to prickly holm oaks that inflict cuts on themselves" (1407a2–6).

Aristotle also recounts a famous case where Pericles tricked the seer Lampon in cross-examination by asking him about the mysteries at Eleusis. Lampon replied that one was not allowed to hear the secret rites if he had not been initiated. (In general, the ancient Athenians took this matter very seriously; the penalty for

4. Plutarch *Pericles* 23.1.
5. See above, p. 18, n. 7.

revealing the mysteries to the uninitiated was death.) Pericles then asked if he, Lampon, knew the secret rites. On hearing him aver that he did, Pericles countered, "Well, how can that be, since *you* have never been initiated?" (1419a2–5).

Plutarch, who lived more than five hundred years after Pericles, also quotes from the oration over the dead in the Samian War (*Pericles* 8.9). This speech was apparently one of Pericles' most famous.[6] He said that

> the dead had become immortal just like the gods. Although we do not see the gods, we infer their reality by the honors that they receive and the benefits that they bestow. This likewise applies to those who have perished on behalf of their city.

Plutarch also quotes Pericles (33.5) as saying when he restrained the Athenians from going out to fight the Spartans at Acharnae in the first campaign of the Peloponnesian War that "trees cut and clipped grow back quickly, but men cut down cannot be recovered so easily." Thucydides attributes a strikingly similar sentiment to him in his first speech at 1.143.5 where his Pericles says, "Don't grieve for your properties and land, save your grief for the loss of men."

Plutarch records a number of other anecdotes and what may be quotes from Pericles, but we have no means of verifying their authenticity. According to Plutarch (8.7) Pericles said that "he spied war storming forth from the Peloponnese." We may note also his remonstrance (8.8) to the tragedian Sophocles, his fellow general at Samos, when he admired a handsome young soldier,

---

6. Plutarch had not, apparently, seen a copy of the speech, for he cites it from Stesimbrotus of Thasos, a contemporary of Pericles.

that "a general not only ought to have clean hands, Sophocles, but a clean mind." When the general Tolmides was about to set off in 447 on the ill-advised expedition into Boeotia that resulted in his death, Pericles is quoted as saying (18.2) that "if he would not listen to Pericles, he would not go wrong waiting for that wisest adviser of all, namely, time."

Plutarch's other quotations of Pericles are more suspect. At 35.2 he recounts how Pericles defused his troops' fear during an eclipse. Seeing that his helmsman was particularly frightened, he held his cloak up before his eyes and asked him if he was afraid. When he replied no, Pericles asked, "How does this differ from that, except that what has caused the darkness is bigger than my cloak?" This is clearly a story fostered in the philosophical schools to support a scientific approach to natural phenomena. Plutarch also reports that on his deathbed Pericles claimed (38.4) as his proudest accomplishment that "no citizen because of me donned mourning garb." These are the all but obligatory last words of a famous man and can scarcely be credited, unless we assume that Pericles was delirious at the last.

The sum total of actual words that can reliably be attributed to Pericles is disappointingly small. Still, to have on good evidence the truly beautiful metaphor likening the loss of the young men of Athens to having the spring taken out of the year is no small thing. It has a piquancy, a "sting," to quote Eupolis, that remains with us.

The Archaeological Evidence

INSCRIPTIONS AND OSTRACA

Despite his prominence in Athenian politics and the leading role he played in the expansion of Athens' influence for a generation, Pericles' name has yet to turn up completely preserved on any of the hundreds of inscriptions to have survived from the fifth century B.C.[1] Only the last two letters of his name are preserved in the fragmentary list of generals who swore to uphold the peace treaty concluded with the inhabitants of the island of Samos in 439 at the close of the bitter conflict that ended their revolt (*IG* I³

---

1. The only inscription that preserves Pericles' name in full is from the mid-fourth century B.C. (*IG* II² 2318). It records victors in dramatic contests going back to the early fifth century. For the year 472 it lists Pericles of Cholargus as producer of the winning tragedies by Aeschylus. This inscription was not seen by Plutarch, and no other ancient source alludes to the fact that Pericles underwrote the production of plays in this year. See above, p. 15.

48 line 43).[2] His name has been restored by editors in another fragmentary inscription, the so-called Springhouse Decree (*IG* I³ 49 line 13). The restoration seems probable, and, if it is correct, about the year 435 he and his family—his sons Paralus and Xanthippus are mentioned by name—offered to pay the cost of a springhouse where the citizens could go to fetch drinking water. The offer was met with thanks, but the people preferred to use public funds for the project.

Two of the largest inscribed marble pillars ever set up in Athens recorded the first twenty-three years of payments to Athena by the members of the Athenian empire; they were placed on the Acropolis—exactly where is uncertain—and are known as the Tribute Lists.[3] Soon after the Athenians transferred the Delian League's funds from Delos to Athens in the year 454, the decision was taken to have each year's payment to Athena inscribed on stone for all to see.[4] This transfer of funds marked a crucial, perhaps final, stage in the league's evolution into an empire. Earlier payments had been made to Delian Apollo and were held in common in the League treasury on the island of Delos. The move to Athens now meant that the payments were made to Athena. The revenue available to the Athenians, and their ability to control it, thus increased greatly. Pericles must have played a major role in these important policy decisions, which increased Athenian control over the subject states of the empire.

2. Thucydides (1.117.3) records that the Samians agreed to dismantle their walls, give up their fleet, and pay for the cost of the war.

3. B. D. Meritt, H. T. Wade-Gery, M. F. McGregor, *The Athenian Tribute Lists,* vols. 1–4 (Princeton, 1939–53), is the fundamental publication.

4. The tragedian Sophocles is recorded in the heading of the list for the year 443/2 as chief treasurer for that year (*IG* I³ 269 line 36).

The tribute money for Athena comprised a sixtieth of each city's total assessment; it was called in Greek "firstfruits" and was similar to a compulsory tithe. The accounts of the first fifteen years (454/3 to 440/39) were inscribed on four sides of a block of white marble that was almost 12 feet tall, nearly 4½ feet wide, and 15½ inches thick. The record of the next eight years (439/8 to 432/1) occupied a second very substantial marble block more than 7 feet high, almost 5 feet wide, and 13 ¾ inches thick.[5] These massive pillars were apparently erected and then inscribed in place year by year. They were as much a visible sign of Athenian might as was the Parthenon. Pericles almost certainly had a hand in the legislation that brought them into being, and surely saw them set up on the Acropolis.

Ostracism was introduced at Athens, it seems, in the late sixth century B.C., apparently as a safeguard against any political figure becoming too powerful. The Athenians did not want another tyrant like Peisistratus and his sons, no matter how enlightened he might be. In essence the institution of ostracism worked as follows: a vote was held in the assembly once a year during the early spring, and if 6,000 votes were cast, the person who received the most votes was forced to go into exile for ten years. He suffered no other penalty and retained his property and political rights. Votes were cast by writing the name of the person to be exiled on broken pieces of pottery, known in Greek as ostraca—hence our word *ostracism*. Ostracism soon became a partisan tool by which to force opponents out. The first os-

5. More than 250 fragments of these two large stelae, or pillars, survive; they can be seen reconstructed in the Epigraphical Museum in Athens. Even in their fragmentary state they are impressive.

tracism attested was held in 487, and the last seventy years later in 417 during the Peloponnesian War. Pericles rid himself of certain political opponents by this device, most notably Thucydides son of Melesias, the politician, not the historian, probably in the year 443. Whether Pericles was much involved in the ostracism of Miltades' son Cimon in 461 is doubtful.

Over 11,000 ostraca have been found in the excavations in Athens, the great majority in the Agora, the ancient marketplace, and in the area of the Ceramicus, the main cemetery of the ancient city. Not all have as yet been published. Thus far, Pericles is known from just two published examples found in the market square.[6] These ostraca were found in different places; one is painted (fig. 1), and the other is incised (fig. 2). It is impossible to date them other than to roughly the middle of the fifth century B.C. They probably come from votes held at two different times. It is surprising, given Pericles' dominance in the city, that more ostraca with his name do not survive. We would expect to find many more, since numerous examples have been found for other notable figures, and it is certain that his enemies made more than one attempt to remove him in this fashion.

PORTRAIT BUSTS

There are four or five known portraits of Pericles, all, it seems, Roman copies of the head of a single bronze original by an artist named Cresilas. We know little about this artist. He was born

6. For the ostraca from the ancient market square, see M. L. Lang, *The Athenian Agora*, vol. 25, *Ostraka* (Princeton, 1990). The ostraca against Pericles are nos. 651–52 on p. 98.

Figure 1. Ostracon of Pericles. American School of Classical Studies at Athens: Agora Excavations.

Figure 2. Ostracon of Pericles. American School of Classical Studies at Athens: Agora Excavations.

on Crete about 480 and about thirty years later came to Athens, where he became one of the most important sculptors of the time. At least three of his works were set up on the Acropolis. The statue Cresilas created of Pericles was probably a conventional male nude holding a spear; it was famous for portraying him as noble, even godlike—in short, in a manner worthy of the nickname he received from the comic poets, namely, "the Olympian one."[7] An inscription from a statue base has been found (*IG* I³ 884) that may indeed be from the base of this famous statue. Unfortunately, the left part of the text of the inscription is missing. It may plausibly be restored to read either "[Xanthippus] son of [Per]icles" or "[Pericles] son of [Per]icles [dedicated] (this statue to Athena). [Cres]ilas sculpted it."[8] If the former is correct, then the statue was erected during Pericles' lifetime, perhaps around 440, by his eldest son. If the latter is correct, and this seems more likely, then Pericles the Younger set it up in memory of his father some time after his father's death in 429. The bronze statue itself has long been lost, no doubt melted down in later times to make weapons.

The Roman copies are all heads from herms with a short beard and a Corinthian helmet pushed back on the head. They are located today in the Berlin Museum, the Princeton Art Museum,

7. Pliny *Natural History* 34.74. "Olympian" in modern English most commonly refers to victors at the Olympic games. "Olympian" in the present case refers to Mount Olympus, the home of the gods of Greek mythology. It is also an important epithet of Zeus, the king of the gods.

8. Letters enclosed by brackets [ ] are lost and have been restored; words in parentheses ( ) were not inscribed but can be readily supplied from the context. A statue base found on the Acropolis naturally had a statue on top dedicated to Athena, goddess of the Acropolis.

the Museo Barraco in Rome, the Vatican Museum, and the British Museum (see fig. 3). The last two copies are labeled with Pericles' name; both are said to have come from near Rome. The Berlin head was found on the island of Lesbos.[9] The provenance of the other two is unknown, although the Princeton head appears to have been purchased in Rome. The identification of the face in Princeton as Pericles has been called into doubt; it does display differences from the others.[10]

There must have been a number of other statues of Pericles. Plutarch (*Pericles* 3.4) mentions several portraits, and about the middle of the second century A.D. the traveler Pausanias (*Description of Greece* 1.25) saw a statue of Pericles, perhaps the one by Cresilas, on the Acropolis at Athens. It seems somewhat odd that there are so few surviving portraits of Pericles. In general, however, it must be observed that few portraits of politicians of this period survive. By contrast, there are many busts of literary figures, especially the three great tragedians, Aeschylus, Sophocles, and Euripides. It is fortunate that we possess the literary sources that we do, because if we had to judge solely from the very few traces of Pericles in the material record, we would have no idea that he was, in point of fact, the most important single statesman of his era, a man who was regarded shortly after his death as the greatest leader of the greatest city during its time of greatest accomplishment.

9. I thank my colleague Professor Carol Mattusch for help in locating these busts. The basic source is G. M. A. Richter, *The Portraits of the Greeks* (London, 1965) 1: 102–4.

10. It is no. 11 by J. C. Griffin in B. Ridgway, *Greek Sculpture in the Art Museum, Princeton University* (Princeton, 1994). I thank Dr. Michael Padgett, the curator of ancient art at the Princeton University Art Museum, for calling my attention to this.

Figure 3.   Bust of Pericles in the British Museum. Photograph by
O. Palagia.

THE BUILDING PROGRAM ON THE ACROPOLIS

Pericles was probably one of those responsible for negotiating a peace with the Persians around 450 known as the Peace of Callias.[11] Following this the Athenians felt free to begin rebuilding the temples that had lain in ruins for a generation as a reminder of the Persian desecration of their holy places. Pericles certainly played a significant role in the great building program that began in the early 440s and continued until the outbreak of the Peloponnesian War in 431 (fig. 4). The chief ornament of that program was the Parthenon, constructed between 447 and 432 B.C. (fig. 5). The architects of the Parthenon were Callicrates and Ictinus, and Phidias produced the great gold and ivory statue of Athena that stood inside. Phidias may also have been in charge of the general program of sculptural decoration for the building.

The great marble ornamental gateway to the Acropolis, the Propylaea (fig. 6), was also constructed as part of this building program. The Parthenon and the Propylaea were clearly planned together, for they are built on the same orientation and share similar dimensions. The width of the Propylaea, for example, was planned to be the same as the length of the Parthenon. The architect of the project was Mnesicles. The gateway was begun in 437 and finished, or at least work on it came to an end, in 432 as war

11. Thucydides does not mention the peace, nor does Herodotus. It is first mentioned by Isocrates in section 120 of his *Panegyricus* of the year 380. And the historian Diodorus (13.4–5) gives an account of it that draws on earlier sources. Scholars have doubted its existence, but the preponderance of evidence suggests that a peace was made at this time. There is a vast bibliography on the matter; see, for example, R. Meiggs, *The Athenian Empire* (Oxford, 1975) 129–51, 487–95.

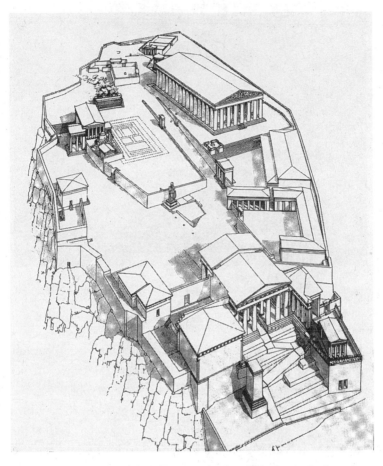

Figure 4. Drawing of the Acropolis by G. P. Stevens. American School of Classical Studies at Athens.

Figure 5.   The Parthenon. Photograph by J. W. Allison.

loomed. The building never received its final touches, but it was greatly admired in antiquity. An entry gate constructed entirely from marble was uniquely impressive; that so impressive a structure was completed in just five years amazed everyone.

Pericles lived to see these two buildings finished. A third building, the Erechtheion, which was located to the north of the Parthenon, was clearly planned during Pericles' lifetime but was probably not started until the 420s. Work on the Erechtheion continued sporadically during the war. Pericles was also responsible for building an odeum, or covered music hall, to the east of the Theater of Dionysus, and other buildings in the lower city, as well as several projects in the countryside. Plutarch lists the Odeum, the Hall of the Mysteries at Eleusis, and the central Long Wall among Pericles' projects. But it is the buildings on the

Figure 6.   The Propylaea. Alison Frantz Photographic Collection, American School of Classical Studies at Athens.

Acropolis (fig. 7) that have universally been admired since they were created.

Five hundred years after their construction Plutarch (*Pericles* 13) described the execution of the buildings on the Acropolis as follows (in Dryden's elegant rendition):

> Undertakings, any one of which singly might have required, they thought, for their completion, several successions and ages of men, were every one of them accomplished in the height and prime of one man's political service. . . . Pericles's works are especially admired, as having been made quickly, to last long. For every particular piece of his work was immediately, even at that time, for its beauty and elegance, antique; and yet in its vigour and freshness looks to this day as if it

Figure 7.   The Acropolis. Photograph by J. W. Allison.

were just executed. There is a sort of bloom of newness upon those works of his, preserving them from the touch of time, as if they had some perennial spirit and undying vitality mingled in the composition of them.

Thucydides too is surely thinking of the temples and public monuments constructed during Pericles' time at the helm of the state when he avers (1.10.2) that if the city were to be deserted and only its temples and other buildings remained, people would think, based on them, that Athens' power had been twice what it actually was.

Thucydides' Portrait
of Pericles I
Prelude to War

The historian Thucydides provides us with our only extensive portrait of Pericles by a contemporary. He portrays him as the principal leader of the Athenians at the outset of the war between the Athenians and the Spartans. The conflict eventually lasted for twenty-seven years, from 431 to 404 B.C.; but Pericles died from the plague in August or September of 429, the third year of the war. He was about sixty-five years old. Our only portrait, then, is of him in the last three years of his life. Thucydides presents him at the height of his influence as a leader.

Thucydides was born at the latest by 454 B.C., for he informs us (5.26.5) that he lived through the entire Peloponnesian War and was old enough to exercise his own critical judgment when the war started in 431. In addition, he served as general in the campaign in Thrace during 424. We know that the minimum age in Athens to be eligible to serve as a general was thirty. He must, therefore, have been at least thirty years of age at the time. During this campaign, he failed to prevent Amphipolis (see map 2) from being taken by Brasidas, the brilliant Spartan commander, and as a result was exiled for twenty years (5.26.5), until the end of the war, when he returned home. It is probably owing to this failure that we have his history at all. Thucydides' status as an exile allowed him to interview participants on both sides as the war continued. He composed some of his history in exile and some in Athens after the war was over. He died, it seems, about 400 B.C.

The portrait that he presents is conveyed largely by the three speeches that he gives to Pericles at crucial points in the narrative of books 1 and 2. Before Pericles' first extended speech at the end of book 1, a speech that showcases him as the leading force behind Athenian policy, Thucydides includes scattered mentions of him by name in the *pentecontaetia,* his account of events that took place in the fifty years between the Persian Wars and the present war (1.89–118.2). At section 111 he mentions a force of 1,000 with Pericles as general that attacked and defeated the Sicyonians. This operation occurred about 455. At 114 he details how Pericles led troops across to the island of Euboea to put down a revolt only to learn that Megara had revolted at his back and the Peloponnesians were about to invade (see map 1).[1] Pericles returned, dealt with the invading Peloponnesians, and then came back to bring Euboea under Athenian control. These events took place during 446. The account is matter of fact, understated, but one can easily sense that Pericles handled most efficiently a strategic situation fraught with peril for the Athenians.

---

1. The term Peloponnesians refers to the Spartans and their allies, who came primarily from the Peloponnese, the southern part of Greece.

Next, in sections 115–117 Thucydides recounts the revolt of the island of Samos (see map 2) that occurred in 440 and was suppressed in 439. Samos had a powerful fleet and was in consequence one of the most important members of the Athenian empire. Pericles' role is stressed in sections 116 and 117. He was one of the commanders in the major naval engagement. He then took a fleet of sixty ships out to intercept a Phoenician force that was reported to be approaching.[2] That report proved to be false. In his absence the Samians surprised the Athenians, broke the Athenian blockade, and regained control of the sea. When Pericles returned, he reestablished the blockade, which brought the Samians to heel. Again, if we can trust Thucydides' account, Pericles played a crucial role in the eventual success of the entire enterprise.

With these brief mentions Thucydides depicts a Pericles who has been a successful military leader in three different campaigns—against the Sicyonians, allies of Corinth and Sparta; against the Euboeans, very important neighboring Athenian allies, and against the Samians, a major naval power and critically important member of Athens' naval alliance. During the course of the second campaign, he also dealt with a Peloponnesian invasion of Attica, keeping the incursion to a minimum. He is thus shown as actively strengthening and defending Athens' empire against its major rivals as well as keeping in line unwilling allies. He has been doing this since roughly 455, that is, for a quarter century prior to the current conflict. While the references are few and matter of fact, they definitely establish his credentials as

---

2. The Phoenicians were allies of the Persians. The Athenians at this time may still have worried about Persian incursions into the Aegean.

an effective military leader. This is surely their purpose in the narrative.

The account of the meeting of the Spartan allies at Corinth and their vote for the imminent war follows immediately in sections 118–125. The next mention of Pericles occurs in the aftermath of this vote. While the Lacedaemonians were actually making preparations for their initial invasion of Attica,[3] they dispatched a series of embassies to Athens to make various charges, thus giving themselves further pretexts for their planned invasion, if the Athenians paid them no mind. Chief among their demands was the order to drive out the pollution that surrounded those involved in suppressing an attempt on Athens by a would-be tyrant named Cylon (1.126). This had happened in the late seventh or early sixth century B.C., so long ago as to be almost a mythical event. Cylon and his followers had taken refuge on the Acropolis; they were promised sanctuary and then killed, some within the holy sanctuary. To kill someone within a religious precinct constituted a grave transgression against the gods. The perpetrators and their descendants were judged accursed on this account and driven out by the Athenians. The Lacedaemonians now revived the charge,

> knowing that Pericles son of Xanthippus was implicated in it
> on his mother's side, and believing that if he were out of the
> picture, matters with the Athenians would progress more easily
> for them. They did not so much expect that he would be exiled
> as that they would bring slander against him in his city, since to

3. Thucydides frequently uses the noun Lacedaemonians to refer to the Spartans. They lived in Lacedaemon and so were called Lacedaemonians, as were many non-Spartans from the region.

some degree the war would occur as a result of his implication
in the curse. They did this because he was their most able leader
and, as head of the government, he opposed at every turn the
Lacedaemonians; nor would he allow the Athenians to yield,
but rather he continually impelled them to war. (1.127)

What better way to compliment Pericles than to have this testi-
monial of his leadership from the enemy? Though Thucydides
does not say anything further, we surely are meant to understand
that this clumsy attempt of the Spartans to discredit him only
gave Pericles added luster with many of his fellow citizens.[4]

These few, but carefully contrived, references to Pericles pre-
cede his first extensive appearance in the *History,* his forceful
speech in the Athenian assembly laying out his strategy for dealing with the upcoming war (1.140–144). It occupies a place of
emphasis at the close of the first book and brought about the de-
finitive rejection of Spartan demands. Here Pericles is presented
as precisely what the Spartans claimed—he is the leader; he
persuades the Athenians. He is, as Thucydides presents the account, the spokesman of the Athenians.

Just before this first speech of Pericles, Thucydides includes
(1.138) an encomium of Themistocles, architect of the Athenian
naval victory over the Persians at Salamis in 480 and father of the
Athenian navy. The careful juxtaposition implies a comparison
with the hero of the Persian Wars and is apt. Themistocles at
Salamis, like Pericles in the great war now to be narrated, employed a strategy that depended on the fleet. In preparation for

---

4. Plutarch at the opening of section 33 of his *Life of Pericles* similarly remarks: "Instead of bringing Pericles under suspicion and reproach, they raised
him into greater credit and esteem with the citizens."

Pericles' first speech in the *History,* Thucydides has led his audience through a careful progression of depictions of him, from capable, even somewhat ruthless, military commander to leader most feared by the enemy to a strategist of Themistoclean stature.

This first speech lays out Pericles' strategy or policy for the conduct of the war. The word in ancient Greek that Thucydides uses for "strategy"—*gnome*—has a wide range of meanings, including "judgment," "opinion," and "advice." It becomes *the* word for Pericles' policy in Thucydides. Pericles' strategy relied in essence on Athenian naval superiority. Athens possessed the strongest navy in the Greek world. Pericles advised his fellow citizens to (1) stay within the walls and rely on the fleet to supply the city,[5] (2) abandon the countryside of Attica to the Lacedaemonians and not give battle on land to a superior Spartan army, (3) rely on the resources of their empire to wear down what was essentially an agrarian, conservative society with little ready cash reserves, and (4) not attempt to add to their empire while they were at war. He says at 1.144.1, near the end of his speech, "I am far more afraid of our own mistakes than I am of the oppositions' plans."

The first words of the speech at the beginning of section 140 deserve quotation in Greek with a transliteration and translation. They are hard-hitting, and powerful in their directness. These words are, of course, Thucydides' re-creation, but one hopes that they closely reflect what Pericles actually said.

---

5. This is a variation of Themistocles' famous advice to the Athenians before the Persian attack in 480. He correctly interpreted the oracle that had admonished them "to trust in the wooden walls" as signifying the ships of the fleet, their newly developed naval power. Others argued that the oracle referred to the wooden ramparts of the Acropolis.

Τῆς μὲν γνώμης ὦ Ἀθηναῖοι, αἰεὶ τῆς αὐτῆς ἔχομαι, μὴ εἴκειν
Πελοποννησίοις.

Tes men gnomes, o Athenaioi, aiei tes autes echomai, me
eikein Peloponnesiois.

Athenian citizens, I hold as always to the same opinion, *do
not yield to the Peloponnesians.*

Thucydides' rendition of this important speech and the events
immediately leading up to it follows. He reports that many
spoke on both sides of the issue, but significantly he gives us
only Pericles' speech.

Thucydides   1.139–145

(139) The Lacedaemonians in their first embassy laid out
such demands concerning the expulsion of the polluted as I
have recounted, and received counterdemands. Afterward in
their approaches to the Athenians they kept bidding them to
leave Potidaea, to let Aegina have autonomy, and above all they
repeatedly made it very clear that there would be no war if the
decree about the Megarians was rescinded. This measure de-
nied the Megarians use both of the harbors under Athenian
rule and of the market of Attica. The Athenians for their part
neither heeded the Lacedaemonians other demands nor rescinded the decree; instead they charged the Megarians with
tilling land that was sacred and off-limits and with harboring
escaped slaves. Finally, there arrived the last ambassadors from
Lacedaemon, Ramphias, Melesippus, and Agesandrus; they did
not make any of the usual statements but said simply the following: "The Lacedaemonians want peace and there would be
peace, if you would let the Hellenes be independent." In assembly the Athenians among themselves were setting forth their
views and resolved to reply once and for all to everything.
Many came forward to speak on both sides of the issue, that is

was right to go to war and conversely that the decree should not stand in the way of peace, but should be rescinded. Pericles, son of Xanthippus, first among the Athenians at that time, the man most effective in speech and action, came forward and urged the following.

(140) "Athenians citizens, I hold as always to the same opinion, do not yield to the Peloponnesians. Yet I know that men do not pursue the fight with the same fervor that led them to the fight; rather, they oscillate in the face of changing fortunes and opinions. Still, I see that it is especially now incumbent upon me to advise the same and similar things as before. Those of you who are persuaded I call upon, even should we falter at times, to stand by the agreed strategy. Otherwise, do not, when we are victorious, claim that you shared our knowledge. Mischances in the affairs of men move no less arbitrarily than men's intentions. So we blame bad luck whenever something happens contrary to what we reasonably expected.

"Before now, and especially now, the Lacedaemonians have clearly been plotting against us. We agreed to arbitrate the differences between us and to retain in the meantime what each had. They have neither sought arbitration nor accepted it when we have offered. They prefer to resolve their complaints with war rather than with words. For some time they have been at us with orders, not requests. They order us to leave Potidaea, to let Aegina be independent, and to rescind the Megarian decree. Now these final ones are here challenging us publicly to let the Hellenes be free! Let no one think that we fight over a trifling matter if we do not rescind the Megarian decree, even though they proclaim that there won't be war if it is revoked.[6] Do not,

---

6. See below, pp. 99–101, on the Megarian decree. One wonders how the Spartans can have claimed that there would be no war if the decree were rescinded. Perhaps they regarded it as a first step toward resolving their differences.

I repeat, blame yourselves that you went to war for a piffle. This so-called small thing tests your entire determination and your strategy. If you give in, straightway something else greater will be demanded, since you yielded out of fear. A firm refusal should make it clear to them that they are to approach you as equals.

(141) "Straightway, then, decide either to yield before you suffer any harm or, if we go to war, as strikes me far better, to fight neither giving in to pretexts great or small nor holding in fear what we possess. For whether a demand from one's equal is the greatest or the most insignificant, if it is imposed without arbitration, it amounts to slavery.

As to the war and the resources on both sides, listen and realize that we are not the weaker. In the first place, the Peloponnesians work the land themselves and have no private or public money. Next, they have no experience of lengthy overseas campaigns, since their attacks on each other do not last long because of poverty. Such people can often not man ships or send out land armies, since doing so involves being absent from their property, expending their own money, not to mention that they have no experience of the sea. Surplus funds, rather than coerced contributions, sustain wars. Farmers are far readier to fight with their bodies than with their money, since they believe that the former are certain to survive the dangers, but there is no guarantee that the latter won't be used up, particularly if, as is likely, the war drags out longer than predicted. In a single battle the Peloponnesians and their allies can stand against all the Greeks. Fight an opposing power that is unlike

---

After all, the disagreements that led to the decision to go to war involved far more than just Megarian interests. The Corinthians, one of the most powerful of Sparta's allies, above all were deeply involved; they would scarcely have agreed to give up their demands just because the Athenians rescinded a decree aimed at Megarians.

them, that they cannot do. They cannot in a single meeting bring anything to a decisive conclusion, but since they all have an equal vote and are from different tribes, each pushes his own agenda. The result is that nothing usually gets accomplished. For some are especially eager to take vengeance on some enemy, while others wish to damage least their own pockets. Slow to meet, they spend very little time on matters of common concern; most of the time they do their own things. In addition, each believes that no harm will come from his neglect, and he delegates it to someone else to have foresight for him. When this same opinion is shared by all privately, the common good is imperceptibly, but utterly, destroyed.

(142) "The major point is that they will be hampered by their lack of money, since they must tarry while they gather it slowly. Yet the opportunities of war are fleeting. Furthermore, their establishment of forts in Attica and their fleet do not need to be feared. It is hard enough in peacetime to build a rival city, even more so for them in enemy countryside when we are building counterfortifications against them. But if they do construct a garrisoned fort, they could harm part of our land with attacks and harbor deserters. That, however, will not suffice to keep us from sailing to their country, building forts, and taking revenge on them with our strength, our ships. Moreover, we have more experience of land warfare as a result of our seafaring than they get from their supremacy on land for seafaring. They will not easily become expert seamen. If you, who have been studying it ever since the Persian Wars, have not yet perfected it, how can they accomplish anything worthwhile? They are farmers, not men of the sea; furthermore, they will not be allowed to practice, since they will always be under attack from us with many ships. Emboldened by their ignorance, they might, if they had superior numbers, risk an engagement against a small attacking fleet, but, hemmed in by many ships, they will lie low. The result will be that with lack of practice

they will be more inept and, on this account, even more loath to engage. Seafaring is a specialized skill, and, as with any other, it does not allow one, whenever one feels like it, to pursue it part-time. Rather, seafaring permits no other outside activity.

(143) "Even if they tried to suborn our foreign sailors with higher pay by meddling with the funds at Olympia or Delphi, that would constitute a threat only if there were not enough citizens and metics to man our ships. As it is, the supply is sufficient, and, what is the most salient point, we have citizens as helmsmen and in the other positions more and better men than the rest of Hellas put together. Furthermore, in addition to the danger, no foreigner for a few days' high wages would find it acceptable to be exiled from his own land and to fight alongside them with diminished prospects of success. The resources of the Peloponnesians are such as I have recounted and similar.

"Our resources are free of the defects I have identified in theirs, and we have other great ones that they do not possess equally. If they attack our territory on foot, we will sail against theirs. It will soon be obvious that to ravage all of Attica is not as serious as the devastation of part of the Peloponnese. They cannot recover their land without a battle, but we have abundant land both on the islands and on the mainland. Mastery of the sea is no small matter. Think about it. If we were islanders, who would be more impregnable than we? Thus, once we have realized that our situation is most analogous to this, we ought to abandon our countryside and properties, guard the sea and the city, and not, upset over property, be provoked to fight it out with the Peloponnesians, who greatly outnumber us. Even supposing we win, we will soon fight against another host just as big; but, should we lose, our alliance, from which we derive our strength, will surely dissolve. Our allies, I assure you, will not remain docile if we do not have sufficient forces to campaign against them. Therefore, don't grieve for your properties and land; save your grief for the loss of men. Men possess things, not the other way round. If I thought I could persuade you, I would bid you to go out and burn your property and show the Peloponnesians that you will not yield for the sake of these things.

(144) "I have many other reasons to hope that we will prevail, if you do not take it upon yourselves to add to your empire while you are at war and if you do not choose to incur unnecessary risks. I fear our own mistakes far more than the plans of our enemies. If events require, these things will be clarified in another speech. But now let us send these men back with the reply that we will let the Megarians use our marketplace and harbors, provided the Lacedaemonians stop their deportation of us and our allies. Neither of these matters is forbidden by our treaty.[7] We will let the cities be independent, if they were independent at the time of the treaty, provided that the Spartans also grant to their cities the right to make their own laws, not under the thumb of Lacedaemonian interests, but independently. We are happy to have arbitration according to the treaty; we will not begin a war, but we will defend ourselves against those who do begin one. These things are both just and appropriate for our city to respond.

"Know finally that it is necessary to go to war. The more confidently we undertake it, the less enamored of it will be the enemy we face. Moreover, from the greatest risks comes the greatest glory for the city and for the individual. Indeed our fathers in standing against the Medes not only did not have our

---

7. In 445, following the recovery of Euboea and the repulse of the Spartans from Attica, the Athenians and Spartans had concluded a peace treaty that was to last thirty years. In fact, it became known as the Thirty Years' Peace. We do not know its precise nature. Clearly a resort to fighting was renounced if the other side would submit to arbitration. By its provisions Athens was to renounce its claim on parts of Boeotia and also on Megara in return for keeping Euboea.

abundant resources, but they abandoned what they had; more
by superior strategy than luck, with greater daring than power
they repulsed the barbarian and brought our affairs to their
present point. We must not let them down, but aggressively re-
pel our enemies in every way and hand on our affairs undiminished to those who come after us."

(145) Thus Pericles spoke. Since they thought that he had
advised them best, the Athenians voted as he bid them, and
they replied to the Lacedaemonians with his opinion in detail
and in whole, just as he phrased it. They would do nothing if
ordered, but with arbitration according to the treaty they were
ready to reach a resolution on equal terms concerning their
complaints. The Lacedaemonian ambassadors went home, and
no further embassies came.

Pericles ends his speech with a reminder of what their fathers
had risked and accomplished against the Persians. He calls on
the Athenians of his own day to live up to that example, to hand
on Athenian power undiminished. In these last two sentences of
section 144 he appeals to the emotions of his audience, presum-
ably very effectively. To have been a fighter against the Persians
at Marathon or at Salamis was the proudest badge of honor for
an Athenian.

The rest of the speech presents us with a man who reasons
with his audience, who persuades by logical argument, and who,
above all, is consistent and steady in his own calculations. He is
in favor of a war that he clearly thinks is unavoidable. He points
out at the opening that the Lacedaemonians plot war against
them. To give in to their demands, he argues, is to invite more
demands. The Lacedaemonians must be forced to deal with the
Athenians as equals. In the central part of the speech (1.141–143),
he considers the resources on both sides. He emphasizes that the

Peloponnesians lack cash and naval experience;[8] in these they cannot match the Athenians. Athens has the advantage and will win, if it guards the sea and the city. Here, in the second part of section 143, he lays out his *gnome,* his strategy, of relying on Athens' sea power. In section 144, after warning about taking on additional risks while fighting a war, he describes how the Athenians should respond to the Lacedaemonians, point by point. The response he recommends is measured, appealing to their treaty with the Lacedaemonians and invoking what is right to do. The Athenians, Thucydides informs us (1.145), voted to accept Pericles' advice as best. They responded to the Peloponnesian ambassadors just as he advised. This is a remarkable portrait of a remarkably effective leader. Thucydides, it should be emphasized, has carefully designed his overall narrative so as to place an account of Themistocles, the architect of the Athenian victory over the Persians at Salamis in 480, just before this first speech of Pericles. The ancient audience would note the deliberate juxtaposition and not fail to make a comparison between the two men.

In response to the charge about the curse of Cylon in section 127, Thucydides reports that the Athenians responded by challenging the Spartans to drive out the curse related to their king Pausanias's death in a sanctuary at Sparta. In sections 128–138 he proceeds to recount first (128–134) the story of the Spartan king Pausanias, the victorious commander against the Persians at Plataea, who was accused of Medism, that is, of being a Persian sympathizer, and starved to death by his fellow Spartans.

8. Thucydides himself argues that money and a navy are basic to power and military success (1.1–19).

He then continues (135–138) with the account of Themistocles, who was implicated in charges of Medism and forced to flee to Persia, where he died in exile. Thucydides sums up Themistocles' unusual gifts at 1.138.3 as follows:

> Themistocles gave the surest signs of natural intelligence and deserved to be admired for this more than any other man. With his native intelligence, having done no homework nor supplementary preparation, he had the most effective advice for problems at hand after the shortest deliberation and was the best predictor of what would happen farthest into the future. Whatever he had to hand, he could explain; at the same time, he was not prevented from giving an adequate judgment about things of which he had no experience. He could especially foresee the better or worse in circumstances that were still unclear. To sum him up, a quick study with a formidable intelligence, he was most effective at improvising what was necessary. He died from an illness.

Unmistakably, these words also suit Pericles to an uncanny degree. The compliment is obvious. Pericles no doubt would have approved. He, after all, had as a young man placed himself squarely in the camp of Themistocles by producing *The Persians* of Aeschylus in late March of 472 (*IG* II² 2318 line 10). Pericles was about twenty-five years old at the time; his father had passed away not long before, probably on campaign. Indeed, Pericles' backing of the play probably constituted his first public act as a politician. At the time, producing a play that celebrated the naval victory at Salamis was surely a partisan act, for it directly reminded the Athenians of the great debt they owed to the principal Athenian responsible for the victory, Themistocles; the play was performed, it appears, just about the time that Themistocles' political enemies were mounting an effort to ostracize him. Despite the support of the youthful Pericles, the Athenians did in fact ostracize Themistocles at some point late in the 470s. The exact chronology of these events unfortunately cannot be established. Pericles seems to have cultivated the association with the great hero of Salamis throughout his career.

I suspect the historian has more in mind here than fittingly introducing Pericles. As Thucydides is about to embark on his account of the great war between the Athenians and the Lacedaemonians, these reminders of Pausanias, the Spartan victor at Plataea, and of Themistocles, the Athenian victor at Salamis, seem somehow particularly appropriate. They had been allies, as had their two countries, in the miraculous victory over the Persians in 480 and 479. These two men, whatever their flaws,[9] had been authentic war heroes, the most famous Greeks of their time. The accounts of their fall from grace among their own people and their ignominious deaths—they ought not to have died so— strike a regretful tone that surely is appropriate to the extended tale of war that will now unfold. I do not mean just the defeat of Athens. If, as I think most probable, Thucydides composed this passage at or near the end of the war, he and his audience knew that an important factor in the eventual victory of the Peloponnesians was that they received money from their old enemy Persia to build a fleet against the Athenians. There was a tragedy manifest in that for all Hellenes.

9. Thucydides (1.95, 130–131) describes Pausanias's high-handed arrogant behavior; Herodotus reports several examples of alleged corrupt behavior on Themistocles' part (taking and making bribes at 8.4–5, taking credit for some one else's ideas at 8.58.2, double dealing at 8.110, and greed at 8.112).

Thucydides' Portrait
of Pericles II

*The First Campaign and
the Funeral Oration*

The actual narrative of the war starts in book 2. Indeed, Thucydides opens book 2 with the following words: "Now from this point begins the war of the Athenians and Peloponnesians and their allies." He gives Pericles two speeches in this book, the famed funeral oration in sections 35–46 and a final speech rallying the Athenians to stay the course in sections 60–64.[1] He also summarizes in section 13 Pericles' exhortation to his fellow citizens as they faced the fact of actual invasion.

As the Peloponnesian invading force was starting out, King Archidamus, leader of the Spartans, sent a final ambassador to Athens. The Athenians did not admit him into the city or to the assembly, for Pericles as general had passed a measure that forbade

1. This final speech will be presented and discussed in the next chapter.

receiving a herald or embassy of the Lacedaemonians when they were on the march (2.12.2). Suspecting that his own estates, which were in the path of the invading force, might be spared by King Archidamus either out of friendship—they were friends—or with the purpose of creating ill feeling against him, Pericles, who was one of the generals, announced in the assembly that if his property was spared, he would give it to the city. He thus avoided suspicion on this account (2.13.1). We hear nothing more about this property.

Thucydides   2.13.2–14

(13.2) Pericles continued to advise in the present crisis what he had in the past, namely, to prepare for war and to bring their possessions in from the fields, not to go forth to battle, but to come into the city and safeguard it, to outfit the fleet wherein lay their strength, and to keep their allies in hand. He affirmed that their strength came from their spendable income and that they would in most respects prevail because of this strategy and the abundance of their money. He bade them be of good cheer, since the city had roughly 600 talents income a year as tribute from the allies apart from other revenue. There remained still on the Acropolis 6,000 talents of silver coinage—at the most it had amounted to 9,700, but some had been spent for the Propylaea and the other buildings and for Potidaea. This sum did not include the uncoined gold and silver contained in private and public dedications, the holy regalias for processions and the games, the Persian booty, and other such, which came to not less than 500 talents. Moreover, the possessions from other temples added not a little that they might use and, if they were forced to do it, they could avail themselves of the gold of the goddess herself. He revealed that the statue had 40 talents' weight of pure gold and that it was all removable.[2] If they used it for their own preservation, they would need to replace it exactly. In this way, he encouraged them about their financial resources. They had, he reminded them, 13,000 infantry, not counting the 16,000 on guard duty in the forts and on the walls. (So great a number were on guard when the enemy first attacked; they were drawn from the very old, the very young, and from the metics who were of infantry status. They needed so many because the wall from Phaleron to the city circuit was 35 stades [4 miles]; the guarded part of the circuit was 43 stades [about 5 miles]. The part that was unguarded is the stretch between the Long Wall and the wall from Phaleron [see map 3]. The Long Walls to Piraeus cover 40 stades [about 4 1/2 miles], of which the outer was manned. The wall surrounding Piraeus and Munychia was 60 stades [roughly 7 1/2 miles], half of which was under guard.) He revealed that there were 1,200 cavalry including mounted archers, 1,600 archers, and 300 seaworthy triremes. These were the resources that the Athenians possessed, and not less in each category, when the initial attack of the Peloponnesians was imminent and they were on the brink of the war. In addition, Pericles repeated his usual arguments to demonstrate that they would be victorious in the war.

(14) The Athenians were persuaded by his words and brought in from the fields their children and wives, as well as the furnishings in their homes and the woodwork that they removed from these dwellings. Their sheep and cattle they sent across to Euboea and nearby islands. The move was hard on most of them because they were always accustomed to live out in the fields.

2. This is a reference to the gold and ivory statue of Athena created by Phidias that adorned the interior of the Parthenon. See above, p. 40.

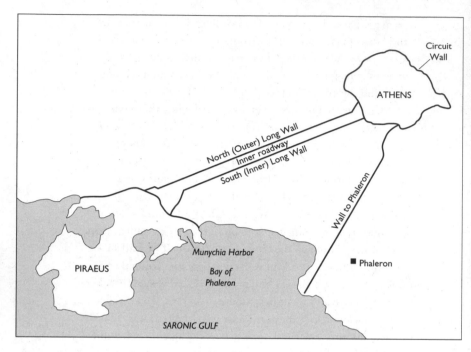

Map 3. Piraeus and the Long Walls

Faced with the actual invasion, Thucydides is at pains here to show Pericles in action. He is one of the generals in the first campaign. He prevents craven dealing with an enemy who is on the move and steadfastly repeats for his citizens his strategic policy, namely, to bring themselves and their property within the walls and to rely on their fleet. He reminds them in detail of their vast economic and strategic resources, pointing out that they will be the winners. He exhorts them to leave the country-side to the invading Peloponnesians. Nearly his first act on the approach of the enemy was to promise to turn his own property over to the Athenians if it escaped devastation. Good leaders, and Pericles is consummately a good leader, do not ask their followers to do anything they are not willing to do. They lead by example, just as Pericles does here.

The Peloponnesian army approached Attica in the spring of 431 (see map 4). Proceeding to the border fort at Oenoe, King Archidamus halted the army for a siege apparently in hopes that the Athenians would yet make some concessions (2.18). After failing to take Oenoe and hearing nothing from the Athenians, the king encamped his army at Eleusis in the Thriasian Plain, one of the places most important in the religious life of the Athenians, and started to devastate the area. Surely he expected the Athenians to come out in defense of the sacred land of Eleusis. Except for some minor cavalry action, they did not respond. He then proceeded toward the most heavily populated suburb of Athens, Acharnae, which supplied 3,000 men, one of the largest contingents of Athenian infantry. Moreover, in contrast to Archidamus's devastation of the territory of Eleusis, which could not be seen from Athens, his occupation of Acharnae was highly provocative, since it was visible from the city walls. His strategy quite obviously was to provoke the Athenians into fighting a pitched land battle (2.19–20). It nearly worked, indeed would have, had not Pericles exerted firm leadership in the face of heavy criticism.

Thucydides 2.21.2–22.2

(21.2) When they saw the army at Acharnae just 60 stades [about 7 1/2 miles] from the city, they no longer thought it bearable, but it seemed terrible that their land was being ravaged before their very eyes, an abomination that the young had never witnessed nor had the old, except at the time of the Persian Wars. It seemed a good idea to everyone, but especially to the

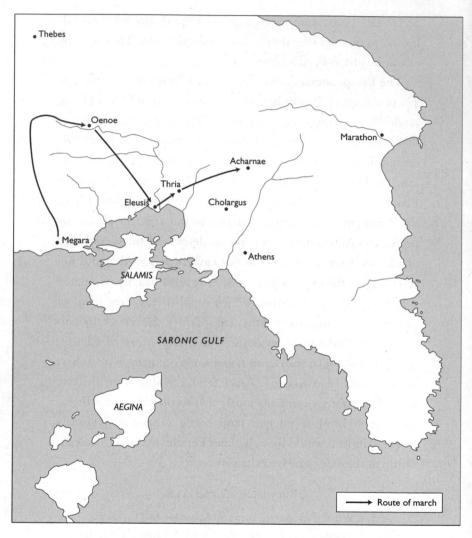

Map 4.   King Archidamus's route into Attica, spring of 431

young, to go out and not to ignore it. Gathering in groups, they argued heatedly, some urging them to sally forth, others forbidding it. Soothsayers chanted many prophecies that each sought out according to his inclination. The Acharnians thought they had the greatest stake in the matter, since it was their land that was being destroyed, and pressed vigorously for an attack. The city was stirred up in every way. They angrily blamed Pericles and remembered nothing that he had advised in the past. Rather they bad-mouthed him, because, although a general, he would not lead them out. (22) They considered him responsible for everything that they were suffering. Since he realized that they were angered for the moment and not thinking clearly and since he believed that his strategy of not giving battle was correct, he allowed no assemblies or other meetings. He kept them from erring, which they would have done had they met in anger rather than with reasoned counsel. He safeguarded the city and, to the extent possible, maintained calm. He had a policy of continually sending out cavalry to prevent raiding parties from the army from attacking the fields near the city.

Pericles is here portrayed as acting firmly, some might say highhandedly, in the face of very heated opposition. As general he prevented meetings that were sure to result in poor decision-making. At the same time as he refused to allow a pitched battle, which he knew they would lose, he mollified at least some by using the cavalry to harass the Peloponnesians who approached too near the city. The result was a standoff. King Archidamus did not lay siege to the city of Athens. Since it was supplied with ample food by the fleet, he knew that he could not starve it out and take it, so he soon withdrew. The Athenians spent the rest of the spring and the summer of 431, the first year of the war, using their fleet for raiding expeditions against the Peloponnesians and their allies and securing allies for themselves. In the late summer, the Athenian army, under the leadership of Pericles, invaded the territory of Megara (see map 4) in force and, after laying it waste, retired to Athens (2.31). This retaliation no doubt did much to cool the ardor of the youngbloods who had wished to take the field against the Peloponnesians.

In the winter, perhaps November, of 431 the Athenians held a state funeral for the fallen of the first year's campaigns. Pericles was elected by his fellow citizens to deliver the eulogy. As a type, the funeral oration over the city's fallen soldiers was evidently an Athenian invention. Thucydides' version is by universal acclaim one of the greatest speeches ever written.

Thucydides   2.34.8–46

(34.8) Pericles the son of Xanthippus was elected to speak over the fallen of this first year. And when the time came, he proceeded from the grave marker to a high speaker's platform constructed so that he might be heard by as much of the gathering as possible, and spoke as follows.

(35) "The majority of those who have spoken here in the past praise the man who instituted this speech by law[3] on the grounds that it is a fine custom for an oration to be delivered over the war dead. But for my part it appears sufficient to honor men who were brave in action also by our action, such as this burial that you see prepared at public expense.[4] It does not seem sensible for the brave deeds of many to be risked on one man's ability to speak persuasively or not. Indeed, in a situation where

---

3. We do not know who that was, although Solon and Cleisthenes are considered likely candidates. Naturally, the Athenians in the audience knew perfectly well to whom Pericles was referring.

. 4. Those who had fallen each year were buried as a group with marble slabs listing their names placed over their remains.

perceptions of the truth are so divided, it is a hard thing for a man to speak in a measured way. The hearer, who knows and is well disposed, perhaps might think that what has been said comes up somewhat short of what he wishes and knows. The one who has no knowledge might suspect from envy that things are exaggerated, should he hear anything that exceeds his own capabilities. Praise accorded to others, I remind you, is palatable only so long as an individual thinks that he also could have accomplished the exploits he hears. Men envy and even disbelieve anything that overshoots this limit. However, since our ancestors of old approved this custom, it is now incumbent upon me, obedient to the law, to make the effort, trying to achieve to the greatest degree what each of you wants and thinks.

(36) "I take my beginning first of all from our ancestors. It is both right and fitting to give honored remembrance to them on this occasion, for they through successive generations always inhabited this land and by their courage passed it down to us free and independent. They are worthy of praise, and even more so are our fathers, who increasing what they received by painful trials left to us the great empire we now possess. We too, the men in the maturity of our years, have augmented the greater parts of the empire and made our city the most self-sufficient in every way for war and for peace. I do not wish to speak at length to you what you know perfectly well, so I shall pass over our exploits in war that added to our rule, whether those we ourselves wrought or those of our fathers exacting revenge from barbarian or Greek foes who attacked us. Rather, the pursuits through which we have reached this pinnacle and the sort of government and lifestyle that have made us preeminent, these I shall first elucidate before I turn to the eulogy of these men. It is entirely fitting on this occasion that these things be uttered and it is an advantage that the whole crowd here, both citizens and foreigners, hear them..

(37) "Our constitution does not out of envy imitate the laws of our neighbors; rather than copy others, we provide a paradigm for them. In name, indeed, it is styled democracy because we handle our affairs not for the advantage of the few but for the many. Even so, by law everyone has an opportunity to participate in private disputes; for public office a man is preferred according to his worth, as each distinguishes himself in something, *not* by the luck of the draw more than as a result of his excellence. If, on the other hand, a man is poor but has some service to offer the city, he is not prevented by the obscurity of his reputation. We conduct public business openly, and, as to the natural suspicion that men have of others' pastimes, we do not get angry at our neighbor if he acts according to his own inclination nor cast at him ugly looks, harmless, but causing resentment. We are completely at ease in our private affairs and are most law-abiding in our public dealings because of fear, paying obedience to those in office and to the laws, especially those that help the wronged and those unwritten ones that, when violated, bring universal shame.

(38) "Moreover, as a matter of policy we have provided the most respites from daily toils, employing throughout the year games and festivals as well as elegant private displays. The daily enjoyment they afford drives away care. On account of the greatness of our city all things, in addition, pour into it from all over the earth. It falls thus to us to enjoy with the same familiarity the goods of other peoples as we do our own.

(39) "In the pursuit of war we differ from our enemies as follows. We keep our city open and never use deportation as a means of preventing someone from learning or seeing a secret by which an enemy might be aided if he got wind of it.[5] We place little trust in secret preparations and deceits, but rather

---

5. This is a direct reference to the Spartans, whose secrecy and deportation of foreigners (cf. 1.144; above, p. 56) was well known, if rather exaggerated.

rely on our own high-spirited bravery. In their upbringing our
enemies from the time they are youngsters cultivate courage
through painful training; as for us, although we grow up in a
more relaxed environment, we confront equivalent dangers no
less courageously. As proof, the Lacedaemonians do not march
into our territory by themselves, but with all their allies. We
by contrast attack nearby territories by ourselves, and, although fighting in a strange land against those defending their
own homes, we usually prevail easily. Because of the attention
we pay to our fleet and because we dispatch our men on land
to many places, no enemy has ever encountered our full might.
Should they, encountering a small part of our forces, prevail
over some of us, they boast that they have repulsed us all. Similarly, when they have been defeated, they claim to have been
bested by all of us. Yet, since we are willing to face danger
with easy-hearted confidence rather than from painful practice, and with a courage not engendered by laws but by our
natural dispositions, we have the added bonus of not wearing
ourselves out over troubles that might be. However, when we
do encounter troubles, we show ourselves no less bold than
those who are always fretting. Both for these things that I have
enumerated and for others I say that our city deserves to be
admired.

(40) "We love beauty with economy, and we pursue wisdom, but with no softness. We accept wealth as an opportunity for action, not as an occasion for boasting.[6] As for
poverty, it is no disgrace to admit it, but quite a disgrace not

---

6. Thucydides depicts Pericles as placing a lot of emphasis in this speech
on wealth and poverty, the rich and poor. The creation of oppositions of this
kind is in part a rhetorical strategy, but it may well reflect the importance Pericles placed on financial resources. In any case, at 1.141.2–5 (above, p. 53) and
2.13.2–6 (above, pp. 62–63) Thucydides has Pericles stress Athens' treasury
and the income from Athens' allies as an important factor in his confidence

to avoid it actively. Most of our citizens can handle competently both private and public affairs, but even those focused primarily on their own businesses understand public affairs adequately. We alone regard a man who does not participate in the affairs of the city to be not 'apolitical,' but useless. In addition, we Athenians can at least judge rightly, if we do not actually formulate, our course of action, since we do not believe that discussion is a detriment to action, but rather we consider it harmful not to be informed by discussion before proceeding to do what is necessary. We stand out in that we are especially daring and unusually able to calculate the risks associated with what we are about to attempt. By contrast, ignorance imparts daring to other men, whereas reasoned calculation causes them to hesitate. Men who understand with absolute clarity both the terrors and the joys of mortal danger and are not on this account dissuaded from it might justly, in my estimation, be accounted the most courageous. In addition, with respect to general goodness we act opposite to most men. We acquire friends not through accepting kindnesses but by conferring them. He who confers the favor is the surer friend, I assure you, because he acts to preserve the obligation due him through kindness to the recipient. The one who owes the favor is less enthusiastic a friend, because he knows that he will return it not as an act of *noblesse oblige,* but from obligation. Furthermore, we alone assist people not by calculating expediency, but by fearlessly trusting our freedom.

(41) "All in all, I say that our entire city is the education of Hellas, and I think that from among us individually the city

---

that the Athenians will be victorious in their conflict with the Spartans. Clearly, money, financial wherewithal, was important both for individuals and for states to flourish. In Athens, however, in contrast to much of Greece, a poor person could participate in public life. Pericles' institution of pay for jury duty in no small measure made this possible.

provides men self-sufficient for every sort of enterprise and endowed with unusual grace. That these are not merely boastful words for the present occasion but, in fact, the truth is shown by the power that has accrued to the city from this lifestyle. Our city alone of all current ones comes to a test more powerful than its reputation. This city alone causes neither chagrin in its warring foes that they have been beaten by lesser men nor blame among its subjects that they are not ruled by worthy men. We are a source of admiration for men now and for generations to come. Since we display power that is witnessed by all with great proofs, we require no Homer to praise us nor any other whose words fill us with momentary pleasure, but whose account the true extent of our deeds will render hollow. Rather, our daring has made every sea and land accessible to us, and everywhere we have left undying memorials of our failures and our successes. For this glorious city, then, these men fought and nobly died rather than see it lost, and it is right that every one of us who survives also toil on its behalf.

(42) "I have expatiated at length on the attributes of our city to persuade you that what is at stake for us is not the same as for those who have nothing similar and, at the same time, to make glorious with proofs the eulogy I now deliver over these fallen. Indeed, the most important parts of that eulogy have now been uttered. The courage of these men and of men like them has added to the sheen of glory for which I have praised our city. Moreover, not for many Hellenes would it be the case, as it is for these men, that the account of their deeds in fact matched their actions. The fine bravery of an individual, it appears to me, death in battle either first intimates or completely confirms. It is generally just, even in the case of those who might not have been totally admirable in other respects, to give first place to courage displayed against the enemy on behalf of their country. Effacing evil with good, they

accomplished more for the common good than the harm they
did privately. Be that as it may, the men we praise here today
did not put off the evil day. They were not unmanned, neither the men of means preferring continued enjoyment of
their wealth nor the paupers by the prospect of accumulating
wealth and escaping poverty. Rather, they considered the
punishment of the enemy more desirable than their own
dreams. Since they believed it the most beautiful of risks, they
wished to pursue the enemy and to postpone their own desires. They consigned to hope the uncertainty of future success and trusted themselves to take boldly in hand what was
in front of them. Thinking that fighting and dying were
preferable to giving in and surviving, they avoided shameful
repute and endured with their bodies the ultimate deed. In
the briefest moment of fortune, at the height of glory, not
fear, they found release.

(43) "Indeed, these men, as I have described them, fittingly became their city. As for the rest of us, it is right to
pray for a less dangerous, but no less courageous, resolve in
the face of the enemy. Consider the gain not just in words of
the sort that someone might utter at length to you who already know it very well as he spouts the benefits in repelling
your foes; rather, contemplate every day the real power of
our city and become its lovers. And if it has a glorious reputation, keep in mind that men achieved it in the past by their
daring, by doing their duty, and with pride in their deeds. If
they failed in some venture, they did not then think it right
to deprive their city of their valor but offered it to the city as
their finest contribution. Relinquishing their bodies for the
common good, they received praise that is ever young and
the most notable tomb, not that in which they rest, but one
where their glory on any occasion of speech or action is preserved eternally. The whole earth is the tomb of famous men,
and not only do the inscriptions in their family plots signal it,

but even among strangers an unwritten remembrance of their courage more than their deeds dwells in each man. Therefore take them as your models, and, judging that happiness comes from freedom and freedom from courage, do not overlook dangers from the enemy. Wretches, for whom there is no prospect of good, would not more rightly be prodigal of their lives than those like yourselves, for whom there is risk of a major reversal of their good fortune if they continue to live, and if they falter at all, their fall would be greatest. For a wise man craven cowardice is more painful than a death that happens suddenly amidst courage and common aspirations.

(44) "For these reasons, I do not weep for the parents of these men who are here today, rather I hope to comfort you. You know that you were reared in a world of many changing fortunes. Fortunate are those who, like these men, meet an end most glorious, even as you meet pain, and those to whom the length of life has been allotted such that their happiness terminates with their death. I know that it is hard to persuade you of this when you will often have reminders of what you once enjoyed, when you see the happiness of others. There is no pain when someone is deprived of good things that he has not experienced; pain comes from losing the good that one has grown accustomed to. It is right for those of you who are still of an age to have children to bear up in the hope of them. Their advent will blur for some of you privately the memory of those you have lost, and it will be a twofold advantage to the city in not being emptied of men and for its security. As to the latter, it is not possible for someone to advise on public policy fairly or justly who does not also, when offering counsel, put his own children equally at risk. Those of you who are past that age believe that the greater part of your life during which you were fortunate was to your gain and that the rest will be brief. Be cheered by the glory of your sons. Love of honor alone is ageless. In feeble

old age, money does not, as some claim, afford pleasure; only honor can do that.

(45) "To the children here present and brothers, you have a great challenge. It is always the custom to praise the one gone, and perhaps in exaggeration of their excellence you may be counted not quite up to them, but a bit inferior. Envy exists as a stumbling block to the living; the dead receive praise with uncontested goodwill. If it is necessary that I also be mindful of the excellence of the wives who will now be widows, I shall indicate it all with a brief admonition. Great glory will come to you if you live up to your existing natures, and greatest will be hers who is least spoken of among men whether for her excellence or for blame.[7]

(46) "I have now said as the law requires what useful I had to say, and the buried have received their honor. The city will raise their children from this time until adulthood at public expense. We award this valuable garland of victory to them and to their survivors because those who bestow the greatest prizes for valor have the best citizens. But now, having mourned for your loved ones, depart."

This magnificent speech is a eulogy of Athens as much as it is praise of the fallen. After a preamble (35) in which Pericles belittles the importance of words as opposed to the deeds of the men who died—one thinks of Lincoln's famous words in the Gettysburg Address, "the world will little note nor long remember what we say here, but it can never forget what they did here"— and an introduction (36) in which he praises their forebears for

---

7. Pericles grants the wives of the fallen this brief mention as he comes to his close; this injunction to them, austere in the extreme, no doubt reflects a widow's traditionally passive role in the Greek world. Widows were to raise the children and were not free to remarry. They had no public role.

the great empire that they now possess, Pericles turns to the main topic of his speech, praise of the Athenian way of life and form of government (37–41). Then he praises the dead whose heroism has made the city what it is (42), exhorts the living to be lovers of their city and to emulate these dead, who have received imperishable glory (43). He consoles briefly the parents (44), sons, brothers, and wives (45) and finally pronounces the rites at an end and invites the mourners to depart (46).

Among many memorable phrases, "our entire city is the education of Hellas" (41.1) and "the whole earth is the tomb of famous men" (43.3) stand out. In the end, however, the speech is notable for what it leaves out. There are no specifics, no individual is named, though undoubtedly some commanders and leading citizens had fallen during the year. Furthermore, Pericles makes almost no mention of any details of present or past campaigns. We learn nothing about which contingents suffered the greatest casualties and where. In talking of the power and greatness of the city, he makes no mention of the Parthenon and the other buildings on the Acropolis, the great building program that he had promoted and that in many people's eyes gave visible expression to Athens' might. Perhaps he felt no need to, for the speech was given just outside the main gate of the city. The Acropolis, then, was in plain view for much of his audience. Even after 2,500 years these buildings are still impressive. Instead, he focuses in lofty, often abstract language on the present greatness of the Athenians, their government and way of life. The delivery of the speech itself was an act meant to exemplify Athens. By exalting their city, Pericles exalted its dead, each and every one equally. To have died for such a great city is, as he presents it, both ennobling and, in an abstract way, consoling.

This is notably not primarily a speech of consolation; it does not offer comfort on a personal level. As Thucydides presents him here, Pericles comes across as proud and austere. One cannot think, for example, that the widows will have been much encouraged to hear that their greatest glory is to be "least spoken of among men" (45). Moreover, right at the opening in his first words (35), he sets himself apart. He will not say what the majority has said on these occasions. His tone toward his audience throughout is didactic.

Thucydides' Portrait
of Pericles III
Plague, Last Speech, and Final Tribute

Following immediately on the funeral oration, that brilliant account of Athenian democracy delivered by the city's greatest statesman, and standing in juxtaposition to it, is Thucydides' clinically vivid description of the plague that attacked the city like an invading army (2.47–54). Thucydides details the symptoms of the disease and its inexorable progression both through the bodies of those infected and through the city. Easily spread, the plague had a devastating effect on the populace, who had come in from the countryside and were crowded into the city.[1]

---

1. Despite Thucydides' very detailed description, modern authorities have not been able to identify the disease with certainty. Smallpox, typhus, measles, typhoid fever, and influenza are frequently mentioned, but none quite suits the pathology of the disease. It appears very probable, in view of the fact that many disease-causing microorganisms mutate rapidly, that the particular disease Thucydides described no longer exists or is no longer as virulent.

It attacked the very fabric of civil life that Pericles, in the careful way that Thucydides has constructed his narrative, had just finished lauding in the funeral oration. People were dying everywhere; even the sacred places were full of corpses—a terrible violation of ancient religious practice. The disease affected both the spirits and the behavior of the Athenians.

> The result was that people thought quick enjoyments best and acted for pleasure only, regarding their bodies and their money as equally ephemeral. No one was ready to take trouble for something that was regarded as noble, in the belief that he might well be dead before attaining it. Whatever was presently enjoyable and anything that contributed to that enjoyment, this was established as noble and worthwhile.[2] No fear of god nor any law of man served as an impediment. (2.53.2–4)

The juxtaposition shocks, so quickly have the ideals enunciated in the funeral oration been cast aside; it underlines with great emphasis both the glory of that democracy and its destruction, or near destruction, by the plague. It brings home forcefully the brutal lesson that chance can wreak havoc on the best laid strategy, even that of a leader such as Pericles. Some things cannot be foreseen.

The plague started at the onset of the second Peloponnesian invasion in the spring of 430. Pericles again responded as general by not allowing the Athenians to go out to fight. As Thucydides puts it, "He had the same strategy (*gnome*) as in the previous incursion" (2.56.1). Instead, he organized a large war fleet in retaliation to harass coastal cities in the northeast Peloponnese. They

---

2. This is a deliberate contrast with Pericles' account of how the men praised in the funeral oration gave no thought to the possible future enjoyment of wealth when faced with death (2.42; above, pp. 73–74).

laid waste the territories of Epidaurus, Troizen, Hermione, and Halieis on the coast of the Argolid Peninsula (map 5) and sacked Prasiae, a coastal town of northeast Laconia (2.55–56). When the fleet returned to Athens, the Peloponnesians had departed, and the plague was in full swing. Thucydides then includes a short account of military events in the north during the summer of 430 and adds without comment the stark fact that 1,500 out of 4,000 foot soldiers on the northern campaign—that is, nearly 40 percent of them!—died of the plague in forty days (2.58).

Thucydides next presents Pericles' third, and last, speech.

Thucydides   2.59–65.4

(59) Following the second invasion of the Peloponnesians, the Athenians, since their land was devastated for a second time and both the plague and the war were oppressing them, experienced a change of heart. They were blaming Pericles for persuading them to fight, and alleging that it was on his account that they had fallen on bad times. Moreover, they were agitating for a rapprochement with the Lacedaemonians. In addition, they were sending embassies to them but accomplished nothing. Utterly at a loss for a strategy, they attacked Pericles. When he perceived that they were angered at the present situation and observed them doing exactly as he expected, he called a meeting. (He was still serving as a general.) He wanted to give them some backbone and, dispelling their angry disposition, to instill in them greater calm and hope. He came forward in the assembly and spoke as follows:

(60) "Not unexpectedly has your anger arisen against me—I do understand the causes. I have summoned this assembly in order to remind you and also to chide you if in any way wrongly you either get angry with me or give in to your misfortunes. I think that if the whole city prospers, it benefits

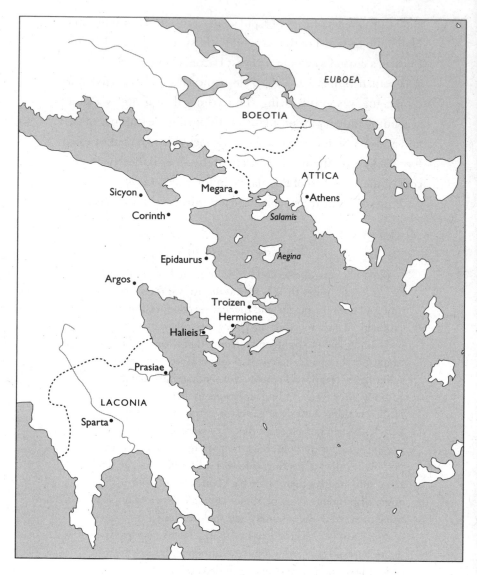

Map 5. Attica and the eastern Peloponnese

private citizens more than if it should prosper for individuals but fail as a whole. For, though a man does well on his own, if his city falls, he is nonetheless destroyed along with it. By contrast, if he has misfortune in a city that prospers, he is preserved much more. Since the city is able to support private misfortunes, but each individual is not able to support the city's misfortunes, clearly it is right for all men to aid the city, rather than what you are now doing. Overwhelmed by your private sufferings, you abandon the common safety, while you blame me as the one who advised you to go to war, and yourselves for agreeing with me. Yet you are angered at me who am, I think, no one's inferior at knowing what needs to be done and conveying that to others, a man who loves his city and is impervious to bribes. The one who knows but does not impart it to others clearly might as well be ignorant. The man able at both, but harboring ill will toward his city, similarly would not express anything with suitable concern. If, on the other hand, he had the concern but had been bought, the whole enterprise would be sold merely for the money. Therefore, if you were persuaded by me in the past to fight because you judged that I had these attributes even a little more than others, then I should not now fittingly have the blame of wrongdoing.

(61) "For those who are fortunate in other respects and have the choice, it is rank foolishness to fight a war. But if it has become necessary either to be subservient by yielding to a neighbor or to conquer by taking risks, the one avoiding the risk deserves more blame than he who stands up to it. I am the same as I was, and I do not change my advice. But you have changed, since it has turned out that you were persuaded when things were going well, but, now that you suffer, you regret your decision. In the infirmity of your thought, my strategy does not appear right. This is because suffering has a hold on each man's perception and no one as yet sees clearly the benefit. Your resolve to persevere in what you have decided lies in

shambles before the onslaught of a great and sudden change of fortune. For that which is sudden, unexpected, and occurring completely contrary to what we calculated does enslave the spirit. And this has happened to you on account of the plague, not to mention other factors. Nonetheless, it is fitting for you, since you inhabit a glorious city and have been brought up in a lifestyle suitable to it, to stand up to the worst misfortunes willingly. It is not right that you take away from the luster of your worth. (Mankind, I remind you, judges it equally right to blame him who because of cowardice falls short of the reputation that he has and to hate him who from too much audacity strives for a reputation that is unsuitable.) Put off, then, your private anguish, and take up again the common good, the preservation of your country.

(62) "As regards your concern about the sufferings of war that they might be great and we still might not prevail, let those arguments suffice by which I have often shown on other occasions that this is not the right way to think. I will now reveal a factor existing for you relative to the size of our empire that you appear to me never to have considered, nor I to have mentioned in my previous speeches. I would not now have recourse to it, since it entails a rather boastful claim, if I did not perceive that you are affrighted beyond reason. You consider that you rule only over your allies, but I point out that of the two spheres open for your use, land and sea, you have complete mastery of the one to as great an extent as you now possess and more, if you desire more. And no one, neither the Great King nor any race on earth, will be able to prevent you from sailing forth with your present naval armada. Moreover, this power is manifest and not dependent on the use of buildings and land of which you think you have been grievously deprived. Indeed, it is not reasonable to fret over these things; rather, make little of them, considering them as a small garden or an expensive trinket compared with our power. Understand that freedom, if we preserve it by defending it, will eas-

ily restore our possessions; whereas men who are subservient to
others usually find their possessions diminished. I urge you not
to show yourselves inferior to your fathers, who held on to what
they acquired by their own labors, not from others', and, preserving these things, they handed them on to you. It is more shameful for men who possess things to be deprived of them than to
suffer a setback trying to acquire them. Swear then to go forth
against your enemies not just in high spirits, but even with a confident swagger. Braggadocio is engendered in a coward as a result of dumb luck; but a confidence bordering on disdain belongs
to that man who trusts in his strategy (*gnome*) to surpass his enemies. This applies to us. Moreover, as long as luck does not take
sides, our knowledge of our innate superiority produces a confident boldness that relies not on hope—hope is for the hopeless—
but on a strategy (*gnome*) based on existing resources whose
calculation is quite certain.

(63) "It is fitting for you to sustain the city's prestige and its
empire, which you all pride yourselves on. Either do not run
away from the pains or do not pursue the honors. Do not think
that you are contesting over one thing only, slavery or freedom,
but also over the loss of empire and the danger from the hatred
incurred in it. We cannot step away from our empire, even if out
of fear in the present circumstance some grandstander with apolitical naïveté made a display of doing so. You have held it for a
long time as a tyranny. To have taken it was, it seems, unjust; to
let it go perilous. Very quickly would such men by persuading
others destroy a city, even one they inhabited independently on
their own. For doing nothing does not survive except by being
paired with activity. Doing nothing has no advantage in an imperial city but suits perfectly a subservient one that slaves in
safety.

(64) "Do not be led astray by retiring citizens who do
nothing nor be angered at me with whom you shared the
decision to fight, if the invading enemy has done what could be

expected when you did not wish to submit and if, in addition, this unpredictable plague has attacked us. It of all things is the only matter that has occurred beyond our expectation. And for this I know that I am still hated to some degree, unjustly so, unless, when you fare well unexpectedly, you will also impute the credit to me. One must face necessarily what the gods give, courageously the work of the enemy. Our city in time past pursued this pattern of behavior; don't let it now stop with you. Know that our city has the highest reputation among all men because it does not yield to misfortunes and has consumed the most lives and labors in war. Remember too that it has acquired the greatest power ever known, and, even if we should now give in at some point (all things by nature diminish), the memory of it will survive forever for our descendants that we as Hellenes ruled the most Hellenes, that we withstood the fiercest enemies both all together and individually, and that we inhabited a city richest in all things and most powerful. And yet men who do nothing would criticize this, but the man who personally strives to accomplish something will emulate it. If someone does not have comparable things, he will be envious. All those who deem it right to rule over others incur hatred and are always troublesome. He has the right plan who accepts the hatred in return for the greatest gains. Hatred, I remind you, does not last very long, but present distinction and future glory last forever.[3] You, since you understand both the glory that is to come and what is not shameful in the present, seize both zealously. Do not send more embassies to the Lacedaemonians, and do not let on that you are laboring under your present pains, for the men who are least pained in spirit at their

<hr/>

3. Thucydides represents Pericles here as claiming the empire as a lasting glory for the living Athenians with much the same words he used in the funeral oration to claim the city as a lasting glory for those who died in the war (2.43; above, pp. 74–75).

misfortunes hold up best when it comes to action. These men make the strongest cities and individuals."

(65) Speaking in this way Pericles sought to disarm the anger of the Athenians toward him and to redirect them from their present troubles to his policy (*gnome*). Publicly, they were persuaded by his words and were no longer sending embassies to the Lacedaemonians but were more committed to the war. Privately, however, they were aggrieved by their sufferings: the general populace because, though they started with less, they were deprived even of these things; the powerful because they had lost their possessions in the countryside with their buildings and beautiful accoutrements; but, what was the main consideration, because they had war instead of peace. Moreover, they did not as a group cease their anger against him until they had fined him. Yet, not much later, as the crowd is wont to do, they elected him again general and turned everything over to him, since they felt less strongly the pain of their own losses and thought him best equipped to do what the entire city needed.

This last speech, which must be placed in the summer of 430, shows Pericles as a leader who is not afraid to say publicly what needs to be said. This was not an easy or safe task. The second Spartan invasion had done great damage over most of the Attic countryside; coinciding with it, the plague had struck. The effect on morale was so devastating that Pericles' fellow citizens tried to sue for peace with the Spartans—a complete rejection of his policies. Despite this resounding repudiation, Pericles here rebukes the Athenians in the assembly for blaming him, calling the plague an object of chance that no one could predict or counter. He reiterates baldly that his strategy for the war is best. The war was unavoidable, the plague unpredictable.

He points out that their naval resources give them supreme control over the sea and that they cannot with impunity give up their empire, even should they wish to. In phraseology reminiscent of the funeral oration, he calls on them to remember the greatness of Athens and live up to it. Finally, he specifically exhorts them not to send embassies to treat further with the Lacedaemonians.

The succinct self-assessment that Thucydides puts in Pericles' mouth (60.5) is notable: "Yet you are angered with me who am . . . no one's inferior at knowing what needs to be done and conveying that to others, a man who loves his city and is impervious to bribes."

That the Athenians in their despair and suffering listened to Pericles at all is surprising and must be a measure of his presence as a speaker. Still, they remained upset; they fined him after a trial that summer and removed him from his post as general. In the next elections, however, they elected him general once again for the campaigning season that began in spring 429. He died in late summer or early autumn of that year.

Thucydides' description of the campaigns of 429 (2.71–92) does not mention Pericles, probably because he took no major part in field operations, either on account of the press of other business or because he was already suffering from illness; so Thucydides includes a final tribute to him in the second part of section 65.

Thucydides   2.65.5–13

For the whole time he stood at the head of the city in peacetime, he led mildly and preserved the city securely. The city became its greatest under him. When the war started, in this too he clearly understood the city's capability. He lived on for two years and six months, and when he died, even more was his foresight about the war recognized. For he said that they

would prevail if they bided their time, kept up their fleet, re-
frained from adding to their empire while at war, and did not
put their city at risk. They, however, did exactly the opposite of
all these things; for personal advancement and profit they
planned things apparently extraneous to the war to the detriment of themselves and the allies. Their schemes, when successful, brought honor and advantage to individuals; but, when
they failed, damage to the war effort befell the entire city. The
reason for this is clear. Pericles, powerful because of his prestige, intelligence, and absolute incorruptibility, restrained the
multitude with a light touch. He was less led by it than he himself led it. He was able to do this because he had no need to flat-
ter the people to gain power by improper means; rather, relying
on the high regard he enjoyed, he could even speak angrily in
opposition to their wishes. Indeed, whenever he perceived that
they were destructively overconfident, he used his tongue to
strike fear into them, but when, on the other hand, they were
afraid for no reason, he reinstilled in them confidence. It was
democracy in name, but in fact it was rule by the first man.
Those who followed him were more or less equals.[4] Striving
each one to be first, they were reduced to handing over even
matters of state to the whims of the people. Consequently, as is
likely to happen in a great city with an empire, many mistakes
were made, not least the expedition to Sicily. Indeed, this was
not so much a miscalculation regarding the enemy as it was
that those who sent out the expedition failed to provide what
was needed to the men who went. They then blunted the efforts of those in the field through slanderous attacks on one another over the leadership of the people, and for the first time
anarchy seized the city's affairs. Even though they lost their
army and the greater part of the fleet in Sicily and there was

4. It is notable that Thucydides does not mention any of these leaders by
name. By comparison with Pericles they are all nameless.

civil strife in the city,[5] they held out for three[6] years against not just their previous enemies plus those from Sicily, but also against a majority of their allies who had revolted, and later against Cyrus, the King's son, who provided money to the Peloponnesians for a fleet. Still they did not surrender until they collapsed as a result of their own private squabbles. So overwhelming and so clear were the considerations at the time to Pericles that he knew in advance that his city would very easily be victorious in war against the Peloponnesians alone.

After this tribute, Pericles is named only once more in the *History,* at 6.31, where Thucydides recounts the sailing of the grand, but doomed armada to Sicily in 415. This splendid force of men and ships made an impressive sight as it was gathering in the Piraeus.[7] Foreigners and country folk came to admire it. Yet Thucydides points out that in numbers of ships the fleet that Pericles and, after him, Hagnon had used against Epidaurus and Potidaea in the second year of the war was not smaller than this fleet that was about to sail to Sicily. Why include this detail at this important point in the narrative? Negative foreshadowing perhaps? Those previous expeditions were not very successful; neither city had been taken, as the Athenian audience would

5. This is a reference to the successful attempt by an oligarchy of 400 to seize control of the city in the summer of 411.

6. The number three in our manuscripts of the text of Thucydides is pretty clearly wrong and has been variously emended to ten or eight by scholars.

7. This famous expedition sailed under the leadership of the Athenian generals Alcibiades, Nicias, and Lamachus. Alcibiades was soon recalled to face charges connected with his alleged profaning of the Eleusinian mysteries, but fled to Sparta. Finally, in 413, the Syracusans with their allies annihilated the Athenians. Thucydides describes the disaster in books 6 and 7.

know. More pointedly, the mention of Pericles at this juncture reminds the audience of his repeated dictum not to attempt new conquests while the war was in progress. Sending out a grand armada far to the west to Sicily clearly flew in the face of the policy that he had so steadfastly advocated.

Here in his farewell tribute and throughout Thucydides has presented us with an overwhelmingly powerful portrait of a leader with the vision, the courage, and the power to do what was best, even in the face of very strong popular opposition. If Thucydides can be trusted, the onset of the plague did not dismay Pericles. He held unwaveringly to a policy that he had carefully thought out and articulated from the outset of the war.[8] As Thucydides presents it, that strategy not only made excellent sense but also would have brought victory, if only Pericles had lived. He alone provided real leadership and had the courage to stay the course. Those who followed him did not have the ability or the will to provide the necessary leadership. Such is Thucydides' picture of Pericles. It has dominated ever since it was written.

Thucydides' *History* is a carefully contrived piece of literature.[9] Although Pericles is the protagonist during the first years of the war, as well as those leading up to it, Thucydides has not

---

8. Thucydides reiterates six times—1.140.1 (above, p. 52); 2.13.2, 9 (above, pp. 62–63), 56.1 (above, p. 80), 61.2 (above, p. 83), and 62.1 (above, p. 84)—that Pericles had the same opinion or gave the same advice; the repetition of this theme is noteworthy, suggesting his constancy in the face of adversity.

9. It must be emphasized that anything in the ancient world that was written for public presentation had first and foremost literary intentions; this is as true of the writings of the philosopher Plato as it is of those of the historians Herodotus and Thucydides. One did not write casually, with the purpose of just giving the facts. Modern "newspaper style" was an unknown concept.

succumbed to the temptation to spread him across large portions of his narrative; rather, he has confined Pericles' appearance and role in events to the close of book 1 and a bit more than the first half of book 2. The concentration of Thucydides' presentation of Pericles in books 1 and 2 gives it unusual force.

To recapitulate, at the close of book one Thucydides presents Pericles in his first speech as another Themistocles. He is the spokesman for the Athenians and the architect of their war policy. That speech answers the final ultimatum of the Lacedaemonians and is set sometime during 432. In the spring of 431, as the Lacedaemonians and their allies were on the march, Thucydides reports (2.13) that Pericles reiterated his policy of relying on the fleet and encouraged his fellow citizens by pointing out that they had the money and the troops sufficient to ensure victory. During that winter, he delivered his funeral oration over the dead of the first campaign. His final speech comes during the next summer, after the second invasion of the Peloponnesians and after the initial onslaught of the plague.

Thucydides has compressed and telescoped events. He has done this most obviously in book 2, where he has juxtaposed the funeral oration (winter 431), the plague (late spring/summer 430), and Pericles' final speech (summer 430). The plague, though it lasted two years and recurred in 427/6, is recounted all at once. It is described, moreover, in clinical detail. The account has special veracity for its audience, for Thucydides explicitly informs us at the end of section 48 that he himself contracted the plague and survived. He rarely injects himself into the narrative by offering a personal comment. That he shares this personal detail is thus very unusual, as well as extremely effective. The impact of the plague on the citizens was no doubt truly terrible, but it surely occurred much more gradually and lasted much longer than Thucydides' concentrated description suggests.

Artistically, the historian has fashioned the narration of the plague to give the maximum contrast to the funeral oration. Each gains emphasis by the juxtaposition. The description of the plague is horrific; its effect on the morale of the Athenians shocks, the more so because it is recounted immediately after Pericles' great evocation of the glory of Athens. The plague narrative also enhances the stature of Pericles. His courage and resolution are not broken in the face of the unstoppable scourge. At the same time, we can understand why the Athenians are disheartened and need the encouragement he offers in his final speech. The entire picture is thus sharpened by the description of the plague. Thucydides' artistry is clear.

How accurate is Thucydides' portrait of Pericles? Was Pericles the preeminent political leader, the brilliant architect of Athenian war policy that Thucydides presents, or was he a somewhat lesser, albeit important, leader whom the historian admired and whose role he exaggerated to make him the pivotal figure? Instead of being in control, was Pericles floundering at the last? Did his own confidence falter? Did not his strategy, at least after the onslaught of the plague, appear to be a complete failure? After all, it was he who had advised the Athenians to move into the city from the countryside. The consequent crowding surely, as he and others must have realized, exacerbated the effects of the plague. We shall probably never know how things appeared to his contemporaries. Whatever the truth, there can be no doubt that he was seen by others, not just by Thucydides, as the preeminent leader of the time. The references in the comic poets and Plato prove this.

Thucydides' account is, at the least, colored by hindsight. His final assessment of Pericles at 2.65 is openly written with knowledge of Athens' eventual defeat in 404, twenty-five years after Pericles' death. Other passages too seem to indicate knowledge of the outcome of the war. For example, Pericles' warning in his first speech not to attempt new conquests (1.144; above, p. 00) appears to have been written with knowledge of the loss of the Sicilian expedition. Despite this, on the whole, the *History* is an austere account that adheres to its primary purpose, to provide a narrative of the events of the war. Thus Thucydides' portrait of Pericles carries great conviction. Thucydides never alludes to the personal affairs of Pericles. It must have been tempting, for example, to mention the fact that Pericles' family was decimated by the plague; he lost his sister and two sons to it. But Thucydides never mentions Pericles' sons, nor, for that matter, Aspasia. Furthermore, he never speaks directly about the attacks on Pericles and his friends.[10] He does not indulge in gossip or hearsay, although twice (2.21.1, 5.16.3) he betrays an awareness of the persistent rumor that Pericles had used public funds to bribe King Pleistoanax to withdraw from Attica. It is to be noted that he does not mention Pericles by name in these two passages.

Though necessarily an artistic construct, Thucydides' portrait of Pericles is convincing, if somewhat idealized. It depicts a man who was without question an unusually strong leader and who undoubtedly led his city into the war. At the same time, the historian does not disguise that fact that Pericles behaved auto-

10. Thucydides does mention that Pericles was fined (2.65.4; above, p. 87), but he tells us nothing further, neither what the charge was nor who brought it and so on.

cratically at times and occasionally used his position as general to suppress opposition. One could argue that since he believed war with the Spartans was inevitable, Pericles had the audacity to want it to happen while he was in charge and could guide his city to victory. Indeed, in Thucydides' presentation, Pericles alone had the leadership ability necessary to control the people. Thucydides expresses this memorably with the observation that Athens was a democracy in name, but in fact it was rule by the first man (2.65). Thucydides must have felt justified in presenting the situation in this way. But, in fact, Pericles did not act entirely on his own; he could not. In the democracy that he led the public assembly had the final say on most matters. The naval strategy (*gnome*), for example, that he so ably articulated was probably an evolving one, elements of which surely had originated with Themistocles, Pericles' father Xanthippus, Aristeides, and other founders of the Delian League. Men of Pericles' own generation too must have had a role in working out this policy, even if he put his stamp on it in the end and claimed it as his own. Whether Thucydides is correct in his assessment that things would have been different had Pericles not died in 429 is one of life's imponderable questions.

Aristophanes and Old Comedy

Caricature and Personal Attack

Political leaders the world over are routinely subject to criticism. It is apparently human nature to attack those in positions of power. Democracies in particular foster climates of free speech, and leaders in democracies, therefore, are often subject to public ridicule. Never has that been more true than in the Athens of Pericles' time. One of the major forms of entertainment was the presentation at state expense of comedies that bristled with explicit attacks on public figures, who were often present in the audience. These plays are what we call Old Comedy. The only extant complete examples of Old Comedy are the wickedly inventive plays of Aristophanes, who was born about 455 B.C. and was very active throughout the years of the Peloponnesian War. Old Comedy flourished for the greater part of Pericles' public career, and he was naturally very often the butt of attacks. Such attacks were an expected part of the genre, meant to keep the great and powerful in their place by evoking laughter at their expense.[1] We may imagine too that these plays afforded considerable amusement even to some of those they attacked. Politicians often have thick skins, even if they do not always possess a good sense of humor.

As a determined leader who was at the helm when the Peloponnesian War broke out, Pericles is naturally blamed for starting the war. In very large measure, in fact, the war defined Pericles. This is particularly the case in Old Comedy, since the war dominated the lives of many of the comic poets for more than a quarter century, and consequently their plays often dealt with themes related to it. They naturally give us a less idealized picture of Pericles than the portraits provided by Herodotus, Protagoras, Sophocles, and especially Thucydides. They often paint Pericles as a tyrannical demagogue; their judgment, in fact, is similar to that of Plato (below, pp. 138–42).

Characters in comedies call Pericles a tyrant, describe him as Zeus-like in his aloofness, and attack him for his womanizing (a common criticism of powerful men in every age). Aspasia, his Milesian common-law wife,[2] was treated very harshly. In Greek the name Aspasia means "gladly welcomed" (the proper name

---

1. Old Comedy may be biased toward aristocrats, for in our evidence it is democratic leaders who are attacked.

2. This is a modern term but clearly represents what Aspasia was to Pericles. See the discussion of Aspasia's status in M. Henry, *Prisoner of History: Aspasia of Miletus and Her Biographical Tradition* (Oxford, 1995) 13–15. Henry concludes that in legal terms in ancient Athens she was most probably a *pallake* (concubine). C. Fornara and L. Samons II, *Athens from Cleisthenes to Pericles* (Berkeley, 1991) 163–64 in app. 4 ("Pericles' Marriages"), more correctly argue that she was his wife.

Joy in modern English is a close equivalent); it no doubt provided the comedians with useful added fodder, at the very least for puns and wordplay. In several fragments, as we shall presently see, Aspasia is called a whore and a madam. The comic poets also took great delight in making jokes about Pericles' head. Perhaps his head was rather large. In any case, it seems very likely that he had a prominent bald pate about which he was self-conscious and so tried to cover up.

In the *Acharnians* of Aristophanes, performed in 425, the lowly Athenian citizen Dicaeopolis—the Everyman and hero of the play—gives a mock-epic account of the origin of the war. The whole thing, he claims, started over a theft by Megarians of some of Aspasia's girls!

> Going to Megara, some youngbloods
> in their cups stole Simaetha, the whore.   525
> The Megarians, bummed and all garlicked[3] up,
> in retaliation grabbed two of Aspasia's whores.
> Thenceforth, the start of the war burst forth
> on all the Greeks on account of three whores.
> Thereupon, pissed, his almightiness Pericles   530
> lightninged, thundered, and screwed up Greece.

What I have translated as "his almightiness" is the epithet "the Olympian." Aristophanes here explicitly represents Pericles thundering and lightning like Olympian Zeus.

Naturally, the ancient audience would immediately think of the cause of the Trojan War. That war, at least as the poets and myth tell it, came about as a result of the theft/rape of Helen by Paris, prince of Troy. The Greeks sent a great expeditionary force

3. Garlic was, it seems, a product Megarian farmers were known for.

to take her back; much of this story is recounted in the *Iliad* of Homer. More specifically, here, however, Aristophanes may be parodying the opening of Herodotus's great history of the Persian Wars (1.1–5), where Herodotus reports that the Persians ascribed the origin of all the conflicts between East and West, between Europe and Asia, to the abductions of women initially by Phoenicians and then by Cretans. "The Persians say that the Asiatics did not make a big deal of the theft of their women, but the Greeks for the sake of one Spartan woman [Helen] mounted a huge campaign, invaded Asia, and destroyed the might of King Priam!" (1.4.3). "So the Persians tell it. They trace the root of their hostility to the Greeks to the sack of Troy" (1.5.1). Herodotus's touch is light; the stories provide him with a somewhat tongue-in-cheek, even racy, beginning for his grand presentation of the real origins of the great conflict between the Greeks and Persians. It seems likely, then, that Dicaeopolis's version of events is a delightfully comic send-up of Herodotus's proem.

The poet then has Dicaeopolis continue his description of Pericles:

> And he passed edicts like broadsides
> proclaiming the Megarians barred from land,
> from marketplace, from sea, and from the very strand!
> And so, the Megarians, since they starved,   535
> begged the Spartans to see if that decree,
> the one about the whores, could be reversed.
> But, we weren't willing, though often they asked.
> Hence, there arose the clanging of shields.

Pericles throws decrees about like thunderbolts, particularly the Megarian decree. Dicaeopolis absurdly connects it with the theft of the whores. As the historian Thucydides (1.139) tells us, the

Spartans claimed that there would be no war if the Athenians rescinded the decree. This made good copy, and so Aristophanes makes use of it, but one cannot credit it completely with causing the war. Megarian interests were only a small part of what lay behind the hostilities.

The decree was enacted, it seems, in 432 and forbade Megarian citizens access to the main marketplace in Athens and to the harbors of the Athenian empire. It was passed apparently in retaliation for Megarian encroachment on sacred lands claimed by the Athenians. Though it is often thought that the motives of the Athenians were economic, that is, to punish the Megarians by excluding them from access to the goods of the empire, this sort of exclusion from particular public areas is usually a punishment for sacrilege. It is preferable, in my opinion, to understand it in this light, since it apparently applied only to Megarian citizens. There were, after all, many living in Megara who were not citizens, chief among them resident aliens and slaves. They probably continued to have access to the market in Athens and to the harbors of the empire and thus could have blunted much of the economic impact of the decree. Still it clearly caused some hardship in Megara.

The scene at lines 729–835 in which the starving Megarian sells his daughters develops from this situation. However, the point of the scene is not to evoke sympathy for the Megarians, but to create raucous verbal and visual humor. The Megarian has disguised his daughters as piglets and offers them for sale to Dicaeopolis, who examines them, sees through the disguise, and comments salaciously on their appearance (769–808 especially). They will be fine when they grow up, succulent morsels for his spit, and so on. A number of the words have two meanings, like "pussy" in English. If the Megarians had really been dying from starvation, this scene would not be funny, but grotesque. Whatever the effect of the decree, no Megarians starved, anymore than they were deprived of land; the comic exaggeration is plain to see.

In his comedy the *Peace,* produced in the spring of 421, eight years after Pericles' death and just weeks before a peace treaty between the Athenians and Spartans was in fact concluded,[4] Aristophanes gives a rather different comic version of the events that led up to the war. He now accuses Pericles of starting it as a smokescreen to distract attention from charges of embezzlement made against Phidias, because he feared that he too would be implicated in the affair.[5] Hermes, who has brought the goddess Peace out of the cave where she has been walled up by War, explains the origins of the war to the chorus of farmers:

> O most clever farmers, heed now my words
> if you desire to hear how Peace was lost.
> Phidias, faring badly, started it first of all.   605
> Next Pericles, fearful he might share his misfortune,
> afraid of your nature and carping manner,
> before he suffered something terrible, lit up the city
> by tossing in the small spark of the Megarian decree.
> And he fanned up so great a war that all the Greeks,   610
> those there, those here, are teary-eyed with the smoke.

4. This treaty was called the Peace of Nicias; it aimed to reestablish the status quo between the two sides but was inconclusive and lasted only a few years.

5. Phidias was apparently charged with making off with some of the valuable materials (gold and ivory) that had been issued to him to use in the chryselephantine statue of Athena, which he made to adorn the interior of the Parthenon. Similar accusations of using war and other events to divert public attention from their own problems have in recent years been leveled at U.S. presidents.

Aristophanes lumps together Phidias's alleged malfeasance, Pericles' possible involvement, and the start of the war because of the Megarian decree. He is clearly making a joke out of things that were probably said, and not in jest, by Pericles' enemies. Yet the hero of the comedy, Trygaeus, responds:

> By Apollo, I never learned this from anyone   615
> nor heard before how Phidias was related to Peace.

And the Chorus adds:

> Nor I too up to now.

Unless these lines were uttered completely tongue in cheek and with dripping sarcasm, they appear to indicate rather clearly that the connection between Phidias and the decree is a particularly outrageous twist that Aristophanes exploits at this point for laughs. Any connection between them, in any case, is very unlikely because the charges against Phidias were probably preferred about 437 while the decree was not passed until about five years later, in 432. Aristophanes does not, we can see from these passages, treat the dead Pericles with a great deal of respect. He plays the theme for laughs, but the barb of seriousness—Pericles caused the war— remains. He implies that the whole tawdry mess could have been avoided if Pericles had been less trigger-happy.

In addition, Aristophanes made a number of derogatory references to the pay of three obols that Pericles instituted so that the poor could serve on juries.[6] For example, the chorus of wasps in his *Wasps* sings:

---

6. Three obols amounted to half a drachma, which was apparently a decent day's pay for one person.

This is the damndest thing to us, if someone being a layabout
makes off with our pay, never in his country's service
having raised an oar, a spear, nor even a blister!
In short, I move in future that a citizen may not receive
the three-obol juror's pay unless he has the sting. (1117–21)

That is, drones—idle bums and parasites of the hive who have
no stinger—should not receive pay. Aristophanes was apparently one of the upper classes who disliked pay for jury duty
enough to ridicule it publicly.[7]

Not every mention of Pericles in Aristophanes, however, is an
attack. The comedian sometimes finds better grist for his mill,
such as Cleon,[8] whom he ridicules in his *Knights,* produced in 424,
as a gluttonous low-life. Despite terrible shortages caused by the
war, the Cleon character in that comedy steals forbidden foods,
bread, meat, and salt fish with which to stuff himself. The slave
comments: "Pericles never thought *he* had the right to have
them" (*Knights* 283). The geography lesson that the scholar gives
to old Strepsiades when he comes to the Thinkery in the *Clouds*
(produced in 423) includes a flattering, and amusingly suggestive,
reference to Pericles' successful Euboean campaign of 446. "And,
you know, Euboea, as you can see [gesturing to a map], lies here at
great length." Not really paying attention, the old lech, playing on

7. See, for example, *Knights* 50–51, 255–257, 805–808, 1358–1360; *Clouds*
863; *Wasps* 300–311, 525, 605–609, 682–690, 700–705.

8. Son of a wealthy tanner, Cleon assumed leadership of the more democratic faction after Pericles' death. He often took extreme positions; it was he,
for example, who proposed that all the Mytilinean men who had revolted
from Athens be executed. The Athenians repented and overturned that decision the next day (Thucydides 3.36–49). Cleon fell in battle at Amphipolis in
422. Neither Thucydides nor Aristophanes liked him.

the feminine gender of the name, replies: "Yep, boy, she really was laid out at length by us and Pericles!" (*Clouds* 211–213).

In his *Moirai* of 430, another of the comic poets, Hermippus, attacks Pericles for his bold talk about the war and mocks him for cowardly lack of action. He addresses him as King of the Satyrs (*PCG* V 47). The satyrs were known for their unbridled lust, so this attack also needles Pericles for his alleged sexual improprieties.

> Satyr King, how come you never
> wish to draw your sword, but brave
> words you brandish on the war?
> Yours is the spirit of a draft dodger.

Pericles' unwillingness to let the Athenians engage in a pitched battle with the Spartan forces (see, for example, Thucydides 2.13 and 21–22; above, pp. 62 and 67) caused much frustration among the Athenians, and undoubtedly there were many scurrilous attacks of just this sort.

Pericles' power was clearly considerable. According to Telecleides, another comic playwright, the Athenians handed over to him

> tributes of cities, even cities, some to tie up, others to undo, stone fortifications to build or, if he wishes, to knock down, libations, armaments, power, peace, wealth, and happiness. (*PCG* VII 45)

As the ultimate tyrant, he has it all, can do it all. Cratinus, however, in an unnamed comedy (*PCG* IV 326), criticizes Pericles about the year 444 for his slowness in finishing the south (or inner) Long Wall that would connect the city with the Piraeus (map 3):

> For a long time now with words
> Pericles promotes it, but he moves it ahead with no action.

The charges mingle, but the comparison with Zeus seems to have been very useful for the poets, for it covered a number of Pericles' reputed sins, both public and private. To be specific, the Zeus comparison encompassed in one figure Pericles' tyrannical power, his aloofness, and his sexual prowess.[9] Zeus's dalliances were legion. It is reported that Telecleides in his *Hesiods* (*PCG* VII 18) said that Chrysilla, the Corinthian, was one of Pericles "the Olympian's" lovers.

Cratinus in his *Chirons* (*PCG* IV 258) gave this genealogy for Zeus/Pericles:

> Dame Civil Strife and
> old Cronus screwing
> produced the greatest
> of all tyrants, the one whom
> the gods style "headgatherer"!

In the accepted genealogy Rhea and Cronus produced Zeus; here Stasis (Civil Strife) and Cronus produce Zeus/Pericles. The epithet translated as "headgatherer" is *kephalegeretan,* a comic coinage of Cratinus that in shape and sound deliciously recalls *nephelegeretan* ("cloudgatherer"), one of Homer's standard epithets for Zeus. It

---

9. It was not a comic poet, however, but the contemporary pamphleteer Stesimbrotus, the Thasian, who voiced the ultimate slander against Pericles. He accused him of having sex with his son's wife (*FgrHist* 107F 10b; Plutarch *Pericles* 13.16). Stesimbrotus's work on Themistocles, Thucydides the politician, and Pericles was, it seems, rather contemptuous of Athens and its leaders. Stesimbrotus was apparently a scandalmonger.

was probably in the same play (*PCG* IV 259) that he produced an even harsher genealogy for Hera/Aspasia:

> Buggery produced for him [Zeus/Pericles] Hera/Aspasia,
> a dog-eyed whore.

Indeed, it may well have been Cratinus who created this extremely negative depiction of Aspasia, which predominates in our sources.[10]

The numerous head jokes form a special class. In his *Thracian Women,* produced in 443, Cratinus describes Pericles as "the onionheaded Zeus" (*PCG* IV 73); surely the point is to skewer Pericles' sensitivity about his shiny bald pate by calling to mind the sheen of onion skin. In his *Nemesis* Cratinus invokes Pericles as "Zeus of Strangers and of Heads" (*PCG* IV 118). The epithet "of Strangers" is common; "of Heads" apparently is a deliberate comic perversion of a cult title for Zeus used in neighboring Boeotia. Telecleides depicted Pericles as "heavy of head, and at times all by himself sending forth a huge cry from his eleven-couched head" (*PCG* VII 47). The exact point of the phrase "eleven-couched" is uncertain, but since the standard dining room had seven couches and a dining room with eleven was unusually large, it probably is a slap at the size of his head. In his *Demes,* a comedy in which he summons up figures from Hades, Eupolis introduced Pericles with the line "You have brought up the very head of those below!" (*PCG* V 115).[11]

10. The opening of Plato's *Menexenus,* if it is indeed by Plato, provides another portrait of Aspasia that is fraught with ironic humor. Despite her alleged activities as a madam, for Plato she was accomplished in the art of rhetoric.

11. Many have thought, following Plutarch *Pericles* 3, that the source of these jokes was that Pericles had a misshapen head. This seems unlikely.

Our citations from the comic poets, except for those from Aristophanes, are scattered quotes mostly collected by Plutarch in his *Life* of Pericles. Because they lack a context, it is very difficult to judge to what extent the poets of Old Comedy attacked Pericles and those close to him. Cratinus seems to have written several plays that had as their primary subject the lampooning of Pericles and his circle. Other references—in fact, most references—were probably, like those in Aristophanes, merely passing jokes.[12] Pericles was good copy, as many prominent political figures have always been. Cratinus and Telecleides put on plays in the 440s and 430s; Eupolis and Aristophanes were active after Pericles' death, in the 420s and later. Even so, he was sufficiently prominent that they could still get mileage from jokes at his expense a decade and more after his death.

These references in comedy provide an intimate sense of the man that we cannot get from other sources. They by no means present an accurate picture, for they create laughter through distortion and exaggeration. Like political cartoons published in modern newspapers and magazines such as *Newsweek* and the *New Yorker,* they are topical and one-dimensional by nature. They are effective, they strike a nerve, because they contain some readily recognizable grain of truth that is humorously exaggerated or distorted.

Elected every year as general, Pericles had a great deal of influence. But he was no all-powerful Zeus. By the force of his own

12. M. Vickers, *Pericles on Stage: Political Comedy in Aristophanes' Early Plays* (Austin, Tex., 1997), interprets many characters in Aristophanes' early comedies as representing Pericles and Alcibiades. Indeed, he treats the plays as political allegories that revolve around Pericles and his ward. This is a provocative but unconvincing approach.

personality he saw that the Athenians did not give in to Spartan demands. In a sense then he did cause the war, but not on the grounds of slights aimed at Aspasia or Phidias. Still, people blamed him for it. In general, the attacks in Attic Old Comedy reveal that Pericles either was perceived or could be believably portrayed as rather aloof, not someone who enjoyed rubbing shoulders with the masses. He was a political leader who could be caricatured with telling effect as a remote Zeus-like figure. It appears that he was also rather sensitive about his head, particularly his baldness. The attacks on his sexual life and on Aspasia reveal that in Old Comedy, as in modern adult comedy, no holds were barred. Moreover, his liaison with Aspasia, a non-Athenian woman, gave the comedians an inviting opening that some of them enjoyed exploiting. Whether in fact Pericles was guilty of sexual misconduct we have no way of knowing. Still, such jokes cannot be made about every man; that they stuck in Pericles' case and were not only repeated but considered funny tells us something about him. Clearly, the allegations were not so absurd in his case as to be totally unbelievable.

Herodotus

Pericles' contemporaries Sophocles and Protagoras, as we will see, depict him as he dealt with the onslaught of the plague, at the end of his life. By contrast, the historian Herodotus of Halicarnassus, who was somewhat younger than Pericles, looks back to Pericles' birth. We do not know exactly when Herodotus was born, but a date around 485 B.C. is not far off the mark. He died around 420, or slightly later. At some point Herodotus participated in the colony in southern Italy at the new city of Thurii (see map 2) that was established with Pericles' support in 444/3. Herodotus also spent considerable time in Athens, where, it is reported, he gave readings from his account of the Persian Wars, which has a distinctly pro-Athenian bias.[1]

1. We learn about Herodotus's readings in Athens from a late source, the *Life of Thucydides* by Marcellinus (section 54). He there recounts that a young and impressionable Thucydides accompanied his father to a reading by Herodotus that so moved him that he cried.

Since in his *Histories* Herodotus has little occasion to mention any event after 479, it would be no cause for surprise if he did not mention Pericles at all.[2] But, in fact, he does name him, just once. At 6.131 he reports that Pericles' mother, Agariste, a few days before she bore him, dreamt that she gave birth to a lion. This is no casual or passing reference. The lion is, among other things, an important symbol of ruling power.[3] Herodotus, moreover, takes great care to emphasize Pericles' birth in his narrative:

> Cleisthenes, the one who established the tribes and the democracy for the Athenians, was born from this union [between Megacles the Athenian and Agariste, the daughter of Cleisthenes of Sicyon]. He was named for his maternal grandfather from Sicyon. Megacles also had another son, Hippocrates, and Hippocrates in turn [fathered] another Megacles and another Agariste, who was named for her grandmother, Agariste, the daughter of Cleisthenes. She married Xanthippus son of Ariphron and, being with child, saw a vision in her sleep—she imagined that she bore a lion. And a few days later she produced Pericles for Xanthippus. (6.131)

Herodotus here gives the family tree of Pericles and his immediate family on his mother's side (see fig. 8). He places Cleisthenes,

2. I have published an expanded and somewhat different version of this in *Noctes Atticae: Studies Presented to Jorgen Mejer* (Copenhagen, 2002) 315–19.

3. The birth of Cypselus, tyrant of Corinth, is likewise heralded in this way in an oracle reported by Herodotus (5.92). In a delightful pastiche of oracular-sounding language, Aristophanes in his *Knights* (1037–1038) has the Paphlagonian slave, the Cleon character, portentously proclaim to Demos (People):

> There is a woman; she will bring forth a lion in holy Athens
> who shall fight for Demos with myriad gnats.

He is, of course, referring to himself in an attempt to persuade Demos to prefer him.

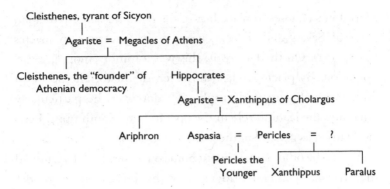

Figure 8.   Tree of Pericles' immediate family.

the founder of Athenian democracy, at the beginning of this genealogical discussion and Pericles at the end. Each is thus emphasized by position. The birth of Pericles culminates Herodotus's account of the Alcmaeonids, the aristocratic family to which Pericles belonged on his mother's side, and their opposition to absolute government (6.121–131). This story of Pericles' Alcmaeonid family in turn immediately follows the narrative of the miraculous Athenian victory at Marathon (6.109–120). That victory was the first against the Persians, whose ultimate goal had been to conquer Greece and make it part of the Persian empire. The victory at Marathon then was instrumental in preserving Greek freedom. Pericles, moreover, has the right pedigree for his future role as the leader of Athenian democracy, for he comes from a family that traditionally opposed tyrannical government; indeed, his grandfather's brother was the founder of Athenian democracy.

Herodotus reinforces the mention of Pericles' birth in book 6 by placing strong emphasis, as he brings his history to a close, on Pericles' father Xanthippus. Indeed, the event of the war that

Herodotus chooses to place last in the *Histories* is the Athenian siege of Sestos and the execution of its governor, Artayctes (9.114–121). On the face of it, this was a minor "mopping up" operation. By placing it last, however, the historian endows it with unusual structural emphasis.[4] Moreover, he particularly attributes the leading role in the operation to Xanthippus, Pericles' father, as general of the Athenian troops.[5]

While the other Greeks went home once they had determined that Xerxes' pontoon bridges over the Hellespont were destroyed, the Athenian troops under Xanthippus mounted a prolonged siege of Sestos in the Thracian Chersonese. Sestos was the most important city on the western, that is, European, side of the Hellespont (see map 2) and controlled the main crossing point. It and the surrounding district were under the control of Artayctes, a subordinate of Xerxes. We are not told his intentions, but surely Xanthippus's purpose was at least twofold: to rid the west bank of the Hellespont of the hateful Persian presence and to establish even momentarily some Athenian presence on this

4. Herodotus was clearly sensitive to the structure of his great work. It can be no accident that this history that deals with the conflict of East and West begins with the Persian empire and closes with the Greeks. The center and turning point, the fulcrum, as it were, is the Ionian rebellion described in book 5, the central book of the nine. This rebellion brought the Greeks and Persians face-to-face in armed conflict. The books before it deal with Persia, Egypt, and Scythia; the books after, with the campaigns in Greece.

5. He is singled out twice in the account as Xanthippus the general (9.114, 120) and is the only commander named. Thucydides in his brief account of the Persian campaigns (1.89.1) simply says that the Athenians and their allies stayed behind and besieged Sestos. Herodotus's naming of Xanthippus is thus very notable.

critical trade route for the shipping of grain from the Black Sea region through the Hellespont. In any case, the fact that the Athenians and their allies stayed in the area suggests that they had some serious strategic goals in mind.

Artayctes and his son escaped from the besieged city but were soon caught and returned to Xanthippus at Sestos. Artayctes offered the Athenians 200 talents to spare his life and that of his son. Xanthippus refused and executed them both at or near the site where Xerxes had constructed the bridges for his troops to cross the Hellespont into Greece. The son was stoned in front of his father, and the father was crucified. Xanthippus then sailed home with the cables of the bridges as part of the booty from the siege. Thus Herodotus ends his great narration of the events of the Persian Wars.

Why does Herodotus bring his account of the wars to a close with this seemingly minor military operation? In giving Xanthippus the final act in the great war that assured the freedom of the Greeks Herodotus pays him and his family an enormous compliment.[6] Surely, however, the historian intends more. The laborious taking of Sestos quite clearly represents the first step in the establishment of Greek, really Athenian, control over the west bank of the Hellespont. Herodotus here, then, explicitly portrays Xanthippus as the initiator of the aggressive policy that

6. When Herodotus composed his history is a matter of discussion. The latest event he mentions, at 7.137 (see Thucydides 2.67), occurred in 430. Thus he was still at work on his *Histories* in that year. When he began, whether he composed the books in order, how much he revised his account are all complex issues and beyond the scope of this study. In any case, I think it likely that he had composed much of his *Histories* before Pericles' death in 429.

led to the creation of the Athenian empire, a policy that his son vigorously promoted. There is, notably, no sentimentality in the account; rather, the historian highlights the harsh work required. Do not be corrupted by your enemy; wipe him out branch and root. In ending his account in this manner, the historian looks ahead, ahead to the developed might of the Athenian empire and to Athens under the son of Xanthippus, Pericles.

But this is not quite the end of Herodotus's *Histories*. In a last coda (9.122) the historian brings us full circle by segueing back across space and time to 549 B.C. to recall Cyrus the Great, the founder of the Persian empire, at the moment of his first great victory, against Astyages, king of the Medes.[7] Cyrus's victorious Persians now desire to move from their rugged land to a more fertile one. He sagely advises against this, warning, "Soft lands love to produce soft men" (9.122.3). They heeded him and went on under his leadership to the series of conquests that created the greater part of the far-flung empire that he handed on to his successors, Cambyses, Darius, and Xerxes. Not coincidentally this moment in the history of the Persians bears a strong similarity to the situation in 479 B.C. of the Greeks, particularly the Athenians, who, buoyed by their miraculous victory over the Persians, are poised to create their own empire. Surely we are meant to remember the words with which Herodotus had ended the proem to his grand account:

---

7. Cyrus the Great is a central figure in the first book of the *Histories;* Herodotus recounts the defeat of Astyages and the Medes at 1.129. To return to Cyrus, to end where he had begun, is a mannerism of epic poetry known as ring composition. Needless to say, the device is deliberate and part of the epic flavor of Herodotus's entire work.

"Of states that were great in the past, the large majority have become small; those great in my day were insignificant before. I shall therefore speak of them all, great and small alike, since I know well that prosperity for men never remains in the same place for long" (1.5.4).

Protagoras

Protagoras of Abdera, the most famous sophist of the age, visited Athens on several occasions, probably for extended periods of time. He came once about 443 B.C. in preparation for creating a law code for the settlement at Thurii. Pericles almost certainly picked him for the task. Plato in his *Protagoras* records another visit about 432. In that dialogue he depicts Pericles' sons, Xanthippus and Paralus, as present at his discourse, which takes place at the home of Callias, their half brother on their mother's side. Protagoras, who was born about 490 and died about 420, was just slightly younger than Pericles and probably knew him very well.

Protagoras enjoyed high repute during his lifetime. He was an agnostic for whom suspension of judgment about the existence or nonexistence of the gods was the only possible course. He was most famous for the saying "Man is the measure of all things," by which he seems to have meant that the sensory experiences and beliefs that each man has are true for that man. In short, what *seems* to each man *is*. By this reasoning, everything is relative, dependent on each person's perceptions.[1] Right and wrong, good and bad, beauty and its opposite, then exist only as each individual determines them. His ideas stirred up much controversy. Plato especially found such teachings very dangerous, for if taken to their logical conclusion, especially in a political setting, the result is anarchy.

Despite Protagoras's importance, almost nothing of his writings has survived.[2] It is intriguing, then, for understanding the relationship between Pericles and Protagoras, that the one substantial fragment that remains of his writings expresses his admiration for Pericles' behavior in the face of the deaths of his sons from the onslaught of the plague in the summer of 430.[3]

> When his youthful sons, fine young men, died within a space of just eight days, he bore it with no outward sign of emotion. For he clung to a tranquillity that every day contributed greatly to his own good fortune and self-composure, as well as to his esteem among the people. For each man, as he saw him enduring his sufferings so steadfastly, considered him to be heroic, brave, and superior to himself, knowing well what his own desperation would be in similar circumstances.

While we cannot discount the possibility that this account is secondhand—that is, based on what Protagoras had heard from others—it certainly purports to be his own observations. If so,

---

1. On the teachings of Protagoras, see W. K. C. Guthrie, *The Sophists* (London, 1971) esp. 181–92.

2. For the fragments, see H. Diels and W. Kranz, *Die Fragmente der Vorsokratiker* (Zurich and Berlin, 1951–1952).

3. See Diels and Kranz, vol. 2, p. 268, frag. 80 B 9.

the passage reveals that Protagoras had access to Pericles at one of the most personally trying times in his life and, since others also saw Pericles dealing with his suffering, that he carried on at least some of his normal business.

Protagoras writes in a prose style that is rather poetic. He emphasizes the enormity of the loss in the first sentence. They were fine young men and his sons. For any parent, the death of a child is the most difficult loss to bear, for children are, in the natural course, expected to outlive their parents and carry on the family line. Not only has Pericles suffered such a loss, but doubly so— he has lost both of his sons—and in the space of just eight days. Protagoras leaves unsaid what everyone knew, namely, that these young men were his only legitimate heirs. Whatever Pericles' private grief—and it must have been overwhelming—he gave no sign of it to others. He kept absolute control of his emotions. It is little wonder, then, that his contemporaries, especially the comic poets, found him aloof and remote.

Sophocles' Oedipus

In the Image of Pericles

Sophocles and Pericles were two of Athens' leading intellectuals. They were also almost exact contemporaries, Sophocles being perhaps a year or two older than Pericles. Although Sophocles was primarily a poet and Pericles a statesman, they knew one another very well, having served together as generals in putting down the Samian revolt in 440–439 B.C. We can surmise, therefore, that both were strongly committed to maintaining Athens' empire. Indeed, we have inscriptional evidence that in 443/2 Sophocles also served as chief Hellenotamias, in charge of collecting and tracking payments from the subject allies.[1] Furthermore, if an anecdote from the Samian campaign about Pericles teasing Sophocles for his sexual proclivities means anything,[2] we may suspect that they not only saw eye-to-

---

1. *IG* I³ 269 line 36.
2. The anecdote is preserved in Plutarch; see above, pp. 30–31.

eye politically on many matters, but that they also were good friends.[3]

The setting of Sophocles' most famous play, *Oedipus the King,* is a city suffering from a plague. The exact date of the play's first production is not known, but it is generally agreed that it belongs to the 420s, probably the early 420s—that is, not very long after Pericles' death. The city in question is Thebes, which was founded in Boeotia by Cadmus and, as the play opens, is now ruled by Oedipus. Oedipus, the protagonist of the play, speaks first, having come out himself to learn from the chorus leader, an old priest, what is wrong. A decisive and compelling leader, Oedipus dominates the stage.

It appears inescapable that the play's fictional plague will have recalled the historical plague that struck Athens at the beginning of the Peloponnesian War and had ended not long before the tragedy was produced. The city was still reeling from the many deaths caused by the plague. It seems, therefore, inevitable that some in the audience will have seen in the character of Oedipus aspects of Pericles. It is by no means a straightforward portrait, and some, wrongly in my view, doubt it completely. How far the character of Oedipus can be interpreted as a portrait of Pericles is not clear. Similarities between the two figures are clear, however, especially at the opening of the play, and warrant consideration. As the play opens, Oedipus addresses the Chorus as follows:

3. By contrast, in his interesting book *Sophocles and Pericles* (Oxford, 1954), V. Ehrenberg takes the position that "Sophocles stood for the Old Polis, and with Pericles began its dissolution" (164). In essence, then, Ehrenberg suggests that Sophocles represents conservative forces, and Pericles progressive (passim and esp. chaps. 7–8, pp. 141–66).

Children, young nurslings of old Cadmus,
why ever do you throng to these my seats,
wreathed with suppliant boughs?
The city teems all at once with incense
and with cries for healing and with groans.   5
Not judging it fitting to learn, children,
from others, I have come here myself,
the man named Oedipus, famous to all.
But, old sir, tell me, since your years suit you
to speak for these, why do you sit here so?   10
What do you fear or want? Know that I
would gladly succor you. Hard-hearted
were I, not pitying your supplication.

Oedipus comes forth from the palace full of genuine concern
for his people. He has not, he makes a point of saying, sent an
emissary but has come himself. The first word he uses—
"Children"—reveals his attitude. With it, he sets himself apart
and above. He reiterates the address "children" at the end of line
6. Line 8 portrays him as well aware of his own reknown and
proud of it. These initial lines show a man of action and a proud
ruler, who, though slightly remote, has the welfare of his people
at heart. He wants to help them.

The priest responds to Oedipus:

O Oedipus, powerful in this land,
you see[4] what years we are who sit   15

4. Here Sophocles introduces the motif of seeing and knowing (the words
derive from the same root in ancient Greek), which he develops at length as
the play progresses. Oedipus, the man who sees and thinks he knows, comes
into conflict with the blind seer, Tiresias, a holy man who does not see but possesses superior knowledge. Oedipus's terrible blinding of himself at the close
of the drama thus holds promise of redemption, of self-knowledge to come.

at your altars, some not yet strong
enough to fly, some weighed by age,
I, priest of Zeus, and also these chosen
youths. The rest of our people, wreathed,
sit in the markets, before the twin temples   20
of Pallas and beside Ismenus's prophetic ash.[5]
    Our city, as you yourself see, reels
terribly now and is no longer able to lift
its head from the depths and reddening swell.
Blighted is she in the seedlings of her earth,   25
blighted in her flocks and in her wives,
barren of offspring. The searing god, the
most hateful plague, has overwhelmed the city.
The house of Cadmus is emptied, but black
Hades grows rich in moans and groans.   30
    I and these children sit at your hearth,
not equating you with the gods, but as
first of men in dealing with life's travails
and in encounters with the gods above.
For you freed us, coming to Cadmus's town,   35
from the tribute we paid to the hard songstress.[6]
And you did these things with no knowledge from us
nor taught by us, but (men say and believe)
by the aid of a god you set life right for us.
    Now, Oedipus, most powerful presence to all,   40
we, suppliants one and all, beseech you
to find some protection for us, either a message
from a god or help you know from a man.

---

5. There were apparently two temples of Pallas Athena in Thebes, and
there was also a temple of Apollo by the river Ismenus, where burnt offerings
were made.

    6. The hard songstress is the Sphinx; she ate those who failed to solve her
riddle.

As a man of experience I think the results
of your plans are likely to be highly efficacious.   45
   Come, o best among men, set aright the city.
Come, take care, since this land now calls you
savior because of your former zeal.
Of your rule let us in no way remember
that we flourished at first and later fell,   50
but with surety set aright this city.
With fitting omen you provided good
fortune to us in the past; be the same now.
For, if you will rule this city, even as you now control it,
better to rule it with men than empty.   55
For of no consequence is a tower or ship
empty of men, no one living within.

In this long speech the priest sets before Oedipus a stark picture of the city's situation. All of the city is in supplication to
him and to the gods. A plague is devastating their city and ren-
dering both the land and the women barren. The city is being
emptied while Hades overflows. The priest reminds Oedipus
of his success in dealing with a previous curse on the city, the
Sphinx, and appeals to him to save the city again and secure his
own reign. Oedipus then responds:

Children worthy of pity, known, not unknown, to me
are the things you have come wanting. Well I know
that you are all sick, yet, sick as you are, there is   60
no one of you who is as sick at heart as I am.[7]

7. Here Sophocles begins to develop the irony for which this play is so
justly famous. Oedipus here speaks much more truly than he realizes. He, of
course, means that his people are sick with the plague and that he is sick with
grief for them. He does not yet realize that it is his sickness, his pollution, that
has blighted his country and caused the plague.

Your suffering comes to each of you by himself
individually and to no other. But my spirit
groans at once for the city and for me and for you.
So you do not rouse me sleeping from a dream,   65
but understand that I have already wept much
and traversed many paths of thought.
The lone remedy I've found, looking everywhere,
I have acted on.

Oedipus's reaction is remarkable. He has just been presented
with a situation that is dire beyond measure. His city faces ex-
tinction from a mysterious and deadly plague. We react to what
has been described as poetry and may well think the priest is ex-
aggerating or indulging in poetic license. The Athenian audience, however, who had recently experienced the virulent plague
that had decimated their city, will surely have reacted quite dif-
ferently. They can scarcely have failed to be moved by a description that must have hit uncomfortably close to home. The
historical plague, it must be remembered, affected nearly every
Athenian household; most Athenians in fact lost immediate
family members to it. Pericles, for example, lost his sister and
two of his three sons. Undaunted, Oedipus assures his people
that he has the situation under control, reiterates his deep care
for the city, for them all, and informs them that he has already put into action the only remedy that he could find after
much thought.[8] Again, the caring man of action comes to the

8. I do not think it accidental that what Oedipus says here bears a fairly close
resemblance at points to the sentiments that Thucydides attributes to Pericles in
the speech he delivers to the Athenians at 2.60 (above, pp. 81–83) right after the
narrative of the plague. In particular, Pericles distinguishes people's personal
sufferings from what must be uppermost, the well-being and survival of the city.

foreground. At the same time, he again separates himself by addressing them as children at line 58. Sophocles also injects another important element into the characterization of Oedipus at this point: he portrays Oedipus as a man who has great confidence in his ability to use his intellect to solve problems. Oedipus has no doubt that he can come up with a plan to deal with the situation.[9]

Thucydides' presentation of Pericles, as well as the portrayals by the poets of Old Comedy, suggests that much in Sophocles' portrait of Oedipus may well recall the real Pericles. Pericles cared for the Athenians, was remote, even somewhat austere, and had great confidence that he had developed the best strategy for the war that was imminent. Moreover, despite the severe problems created by the onset of the plague, he persevered; he remained steadfast in his belief that they would prevail.

It is fitting that Sophocles places this partial portrait of Athens' great leader in the foreground of a drama that seems to be designed more generally to remind Athenians that man is not, as Protagoras had claimed, "the measure of all things," but, rather, that there are things in the universe beyond or greater than mortal men. The play was, of course, performed at a religious festival.[10] Moreover, we gather from Thucydides' account that, although Pericles had great confidence in his carefully calculated strategy for the war, he also understood that chance and

9. Sophocles portrays Pericles' self-possession and self-confidence by having him use the first-person pronoun *I* frequently in these opening lines.

10. All Greek tragedies and comedies were performed at religious festivals; the main festival at which tragedies in Athens were presented was the Dionysia, a festival in honor of the god Dionysus.

the unforeseen played a significant role in human affairs.[11] The disastrous plague of 430 certainly taught him this, if he had not come to understand it long before. Similarly, Oedipus, who is depicted as supremely confident that he knows and understands the situation, learns during the course of the play that his knowledge is disastrously faulty. Ultimately, of course, Oedipus learns that, no matter how hard he tries, man cannot change what fate and the gods have ordained.

The theme that man is subordinate to the divine, that human knowledge does not always suffice, is not a new one for Sophocles. In 442, approximately fourteen years prior to *Oedipus the King,* Sophocles had presented his play *Antigone.* In it he portrays Creon as a leader newly come to power who becomes intransigent when faced with any opposition and who is determined that his edicts will be obeyed. Creon ignores his niece Antigone's claims that divine law sanctions the burial of her brother, and brutally refuses to recognize the power of the love that binds his son Haemon to Antigone, who is his betrothed. Creon's intransigence causes the deaths of both Haemon and Antigone and results also in the suicide of his wife. At the end of the play he has engulfed himself in tragedy and destroyed those whom he loved most. His confidence in his own power and his denial of the divine order bring about his destruction. While it can be argued that Sophocles is engaging here in criticism of Pericles and his rationalist ideas (and some in his audience may have taken away this message),[12] there is little in

---

11. Thucydides 1.140.1 (above, p. 52), 2.61.3 (above, p. 84), 64.1–2 (above, p. 86).

12. Ehrenberg, *Sophocles and Pericles,* argues that Sophocles is criticizing Pericles here, and sees the two men as engaged in a basic conflict of ideas.

the portrait of this rather ordinary, extremely insecure ruler to suggest that anyone was meant to see Pericles behind the character of Creon.[13] Rather, Sophocles seems to direct his criticism in *Antigone* and *Oedipus the King* more widely at all those who believed that human reason could adequately explain and account for everything. Surely, in addition to any number of political leaders, he also has in mind serious philosophical thinkers, such as Protagoras, and natural scientists, such as Anaxagoras, not to mention traveling teachers of rhetoric, such as Gorgias, who promised for a fee to teach persuasive speech, goodness, and so on.

13. See, for example, Mark Griffith, *Sophocles Antigone* (Cambridge, 1999) 35: "He [Creon] is presented as a well-meaning, unexceptional man, fatally corrupted and ruined by the exigencies of power."

Lysias, Xenophon, and Plato

The life of the speechwriter Lysias straddled the fifth and
fourth centuries B.C. Born about 450 B.C., in his formative years
he must have been aware of Pericles, whether he personally had
direct contact with him or not. Lysias did not begin producing
speeches until about thirty years after Pericles' death.[1] In his
speech *Against Eratosthenes* (4) he tells us that "Cephalus, my father, was persuaded by Pericles to come to Athens"; so his father
at least had some personal acquaintance with Pericles. Lysias's
wealthy mercantile family was from the city of Syracuse in
Sicily and acquired metic or resident alien status in Athens.

Like Herodotus, Lysias is said to have gone out to the colony
at Thurii. He probably did not take part in the original settlement of 444/3, when he would have been just a child, but went

---

1. Lysias and other professional speechwriters composed speeches for private citizens to use in the law courts. In Athens a person prosecuted or de-
fended on his own without attorneys.

to Thurii in 430/29, when he was about twenty, perhaps to escape the sufferings caused by the plague in Athens. He and his brother, Polemarchus, returned to Athens in 412/11, where they flourished as weapons makers. In 403, however, the Thirty summarily arrested them for no other reason than to seize their substantial assets.[2] Lysias escaped, but Polemarchus was executed.

Other than the mention in *Against Eratosthenes,* Lysias names Pericles just twice elsewhere, each time to hold him up as an exemplar to Athenians of his own day. In his speech *Against Andocides* (10) Lysias turns to Pericles for a precedent: "Men say that Pericles urged you concerning those who blaspheme to use not only the written laws but also the unwritten ones." Note that Thucydides also has Pericles mention the powerful force of unwritten laws in the funeral oration.[3] It appears likely that Pericles in fact was fond of calling on the authority of those unwritten laws that govern proper human behavior. Finally, in his *Against Nicomachus* (28), Lysias places Pericles among the great lawgivers of the past and contrasts him with the low-lifes to whom the Athenians were now entrusting the city's affairs: "Our ancestors used to choose as lawgivers Solon, Themistocles, and Pericles,

---

2. After the defeat of Athens at the hands of the Spartans in the spring of 404, an oligarchy of thirty (the Thirty) was imposed. They rewrote the laws, removed democratic opponents, and then purged many respectable citizens and resident aliens. They were in fact referred to as the Thirty Tyrants, so harsh was their regime (Xenophon *Hellenica* 2.3.16, 4.1; Aristotle *Rhetoric* 1401a). Early in 403 the democrats mounted armed opposition, and by September of the same year, after some bloody fighting and Spartan intervention, democracy was restored.

3. See the end of section 37 in book 2 of Thucydides; above, p. 70.

thinking that laws will be like the men who make them."[4] Instead of an actual historical person, Pericles has become already in Lysias a paradigm, a mythic "great" figure of the past.

By contrast, neither Xenophon nor Plato, whose prolific writing careers date to the first half of the fourth century B.C., can have known Pericles personally. Born in 430 B.C., Xenophon was about a year old when Pericles died; Plato was born the next year, the year of Pericles' death. However, both men grew up in wealthy Athenian families and certainly had considerable contact with people who had intimate knowledge of Pericles. Both, for example, knew Pericles the Younger, Pericles' son by Aspasia.[5] Each in his formative years was also a follower of Socrates, whose circle included Pericles' ward Alcibiades.

Neither of these writers makes Pericles the main subject of any of his works, but each names him a number of times in passing. Xenophon twice mentions him or, rather, records Socrates as mentioning him, both times in the same breath as Themistocles. Socrates remarks that both men made the city love them, Pericles with spells, that is, with his charm and charisma, Themistocles by applying something good to the city, namely, the fleet (*Memorabilia* 2.6.13). Similarly, Socrates advises Callias that, if he wants to win his young friend Autolycus's favor, he should attempt to discover what knowledge Themistocles had that en-

---

4. Note the juxtapostion of Themistocles and Pericles.

5. Pericles the Younger was born about 440 and was one of the generals at the time of the sea battle at Arginousae (406 B.C.); tragically, he was one of the six generals executed after the battle (Xenophon *Hellenica* 1.5.16, 7.2–35). When Pericles' two legitimate sons, Paralus and Xanthippus, died of the plague in 430, Pericles approached the assembly and obtained citizenship for Pericles the Younger.

abled him to free Greece and what Pericles knew that made him the city's best adviser (*Symposium* 8.39).

In the opening sections of the *Memorabilia* Xenophon seeks to defend Socrates against the charges laid against him, mainly those of impiety and of corrupting the youth of the city.[6] He particularly seeks to dispel the charge that Socrates had been a bad influence on Critias and Alcibiades, two who were notoriously involved in alleged acts of impiety and whose later actions contributed greatly to the troubles of the city. Critias, for example, was implicated in the incident of the mutilation of the herms in 415 and became one of the Thirty Tyrants after Athens' defeat in 404.[7] A relative of Plato, he was leader of the extremists and was killed fighting in the spring of 403. Alcibiades seems not to have been involved in the desecration of the herms. The main accusation against him, however, was more serious, namely, that he had burlesqued the secret rites of the Eleusinian mysteries at a party in a private house. The penalty for revealing these rites to the uninitiated was death. Even though he was a general of the expedition, he was recalled on his way to Sicily to face charges of impiety. Thereupon, he fled to Sparta, where he advised the Spartans to send one of their own generals to Syracuse and to establish a fort year-round in Attica. This they did, and these actions contributed significantly to the eventual defeat of the Athenians.

6. See also the very similar summary of charges provided by Plato in the *Apology* (24b8–c1): "Socrates does wrong by corrupting the youth and not believing in the gods that the city worships but in other, newfangled ones."

7. Herms, essentially pillars with heads and genitals, were statues sacred to Hermes, god of wayfarers, and stood outside houses on the road. Apparently a group opposed to the expedition to Sicily mutilated them in an attempt to forestall its sailing.

Xenophon does not deny that Critias and Alcibiades associated with Socrates; rather, he points out that from the first both
men were politically very ambitious. They preferred to converse
with those they perceived as powerful, namely, with the leading
politicians. Thus Socrates, a thinker who was notorious for taking almost no part in politics, can have exercised little real influence over them. In support of this position, Xenophon recounts
the following conversation between Alcibiades and Pericles. It
is certainly made up for inclusion in the *Memorabilia*. Whether
it reflects the gist of real discussions between the two men, we
have no way of knowing.

Memorabilia 1.2.40–46

It is reported that before he was twenty years of age Alcibiades had the following discussion concerning laws with Pericles, his guardian and the leader of the city.

"Tell me," he said, "Pericles, could you instruct me what is a
law?"

"Why, of course," Pericles responded.

"By the gods, then, teach me," said Alcibiades, "for I have
heard certain ones receiving praise as men of law, but I think
no one rightly deserves that praise if he does not know what a
law is." [Alcibiades is clearly baiting his guardian, for it is clear
that Pericles is one of those he has heard praised as a man of
law.]

"Alcibiades, it is not at all a difficult matter that you desire
when you wish to know what a law is. The laws are all those
measures that the people deliberating together have written
prescribing what it is necessary to do and what is forbidden."

"Do the people when legislating believe that it is necessary
to do good or evil?"

"Why, good, by Zeus, young man," he said, "never evil."

"If it is not the people, as in the case where there is an oligarchy, but the few deliberating together that enact what ought to be done, what are these?"

"Everything," he replied, "that the ruling power in a state has enacted after due deliberation as right to do is called law."

"Then if a tyrant ruling a city prescribes for the citizens what it is right to do, are these measures also laws?"

"Even as many measures as a ruling tyrant prescribes," Pericles replied, "these too are called laws."

"Violence and lawlessness," Alcibiades continued, "what are they, Pericles? Do they not obtain whenever the more powerful individual makes the weaker man do his will, not by persuasion, but by force?"

"I agree," Pericles responded.

"Then as many things as a tyrant prescribes for his citizens without persuading them, this is lawlessness, is it not?"

"It seems so," Pericles agreed. "I retract my statement that whatever a tyrant prescribes without persuasion is law."

"And what about the measures that the few prescribe, not persuading the many, but by being more powerful? Are we to say this is violence or not?"

"It seems to me," Pericles responded, "that everything that someone forces someone else to do, not using persuasion, whether he enacts it or not, is violence rather than law."

"Then whatever the people as a whole, being more powerful than the wealthy, enact without the use of persuasion, this too would count as violence rather than law?"

"Alcibiades," Pericles cut in, "I too when I was your age was very smart when it came to such debates. For we practiced the same sort of things you now clearly study, and we too liked splitting hairs."

Alcibiades rejoined, "Would that I had known you then, Pericles, when you were at the height of your powers in these matters!"

Alcibiades was born about 450 B.C., so this fictional conversation is imagined as occurring in the first years of the war and not long before Pericles' death. This setting gives a verisimilitude to Pericles' indulgent and world-weary attitude. Alcibiades' cheeky, if not very subtle, attempt to show up his guardian perfectly illustrates the point Xenophon is after. Such a young man, if he could behave so audaciously toward the most powerful and respected man in the city, would scarcely have taken a dreamer like Socrates seriously. For Xenophon, Pericles was quite clearly the greatest Athenian statesman of the second half of the fifth century B.C.

Plato presents us with a far more complex situation. He certainly was one of the most serious thinkers in history; he was also one of mankind's greatest writers. He is not easy to interpret. Each of his dialogues is a subtle masterpiece of character drawing where surface meaning is often undercut by playful irony.

Plato exploits the themes of Pericles as great orator and politician but does so in his characteristically ironic way. In the *Symposium,* for example, Plato has Alcibiades humorously praise Socrates as a uniquely persuasive speaker and wise man. Although he, Alcibiades, has heard Pericles and other great speakers, none, he claims, has affected him the way Socrates does (215e4). There is no human yardstick, he avers a bit later (221c8), against which to compare Socrates, whereas you can compare a Pericles to Nestor and Antenor, proverbially good speakers and wise men in Homer.

In the playful introduction to the *Menexenus,* Socrates recounts for Menexenus a funeral speech supposedly composed by

Aspasia,[8] who, he reports, has made many men good orators, above all Pericles (235e6). And by the way, he divulges, it was she who put together that funeral speech for him (236b5)![9] Similarly, in a passage in the *Protagoras* (329a) in which Plato has Socrates criticize orators for their set speeches as opposed to those, like himself, who indulge in question and answer, he singles out Pericles: "You might hear this sort of speech from Pericles or one of the other powerful speakers." Plato thus both acknowledges Pericles' preeminence as an orator and pokes fun at such speakers.

In another important passage near the close of the *Phaedrus* (269c6–270b), Phaedrus asks Socrates where a person might acquire the art of true rhetoric and persuasion.[10] Socrates responds that one must be a natural orator and supplement that with knowledge and practice. Pericles, he adds archly, came as close as anyone to being the most perfect at oratory.

> All great arts require endless prating and lofty theorizing concerning nature. For it is likely that the requisite high-mindedness and perfection in everything derives from these activities. And Pericles acquired them in addition to his natural talent. For, falling in with Anaxagoras, who talked incessantly about such things, he was filled full of lofty theorizing and came to the nature of mind and mindlessness. From all this he drew what was useful for the art of speaking. (270a)

8. Menexenus was one of Socrates' young followers who is represented in the *Phaedo* (59b9) as present at Socrates' death.

9. This is almost certainly a reference to the funeral oration in Thucydides' *History*.

10. Phaedrus was a member of Socrates' circle and one of the speakers in Plato's *Symposium* (178a–180b). Born about 450, he was about the same age as Alcibiades.

This is transparently uttered tongue-in-cheek, even though Pericles does in fact appear to have been quite close to Anaxagoras. Plato elsewhere (*Alcibiades* I 118c), for example, reports that Pericles associated with Anaxagoras, and Isocrates (*Antidosis* 235) says that he was a student of Anaxagoras. However, the mention of Anaxagoras in this passage from the *Phaedrus* is very deliberate: he was one of the Ionian philosophers who speculated about the physical nature of the universe. In addition, he believed that the material world was controlled in some way by something he called *nous* (mind). Thus by associating with him Pericles in some fashion got to know the nature of mind and its opposite! Socrates here is made to joke about one of Anaxagoras's basic ideas.[11] Moreover, the word used twice in this passage for lofty theorizing is *meteorologia,* which refers to the study of phenomena in the upper air. Although Socrates was lampooned by Aristophanes for engaging in such studies,[12] we know in fact that he did not believe that much insight about the human soul

11. Note also what Socrates says about Anaxagoras in this exchange with Meletus, his main accuser, in the *Apology* (26d–e): "O amazing Meletus, why do you say these things? Do I not believe that the sun and the moon are gods, just as the rest of mankind does?" "By Zeus, jurymen, no, since he believes that the sun is a rock and the moon earth." "Dear Meletus, do you think you are accusing Anaxagoras? And do you so despise the jurymen here and think them so unlettered that they don't know that the books of the Clazomenian Anaxagoras fairly groan with the weight of such arguments?"

12. See Aristophanes *Clouds.* especially Socrates' initial entrance at lines 215–274; see also Plato *Apology* 19c2–4: "You yourselves have seen these things in that comedy of Aristophanes, some Socrates or other being whisked about claiming that he walks on the air and uttering much other tomfoolery."

could be gained from them.[13] Good as Pericles was as a speaker, then, the passage fairly brims with ironic humor. Plato does not seriously represent Socrates as holding the view that Pericles had learned what was really needed from Anaxagoras.

Plato himself was very interested in human behavior, especially the problem of how men influence one another—for example, how parents influence their children, what can be taught, and who are the best teachers. Much of his writing deals, in one way or another, with these themes. Pericles interested him greatly in this regard, for Pericles' two legitimate sons, Paralus and Xanthippus, apparently had none of their father's abilities. Indeed, they were perhaps notoriously lacking.[14] Thus at times in Plato (*Protagoras* 319e and *Meno* 94b) Pericles exemplifies a paradox that we still recognize: namely, why is it that great men rarely produce outstanding sons or daughters? Athenian leaders in particular, Plato points out, have not been able to pass down their excellence to their sons.

In a number of passages Plato, like Lysias and Xenophon, couples Pericles with Themistocles and others in the pantheon of great Athenian politicians.[15] In doing this they all accept the tradition that Pericles himself began in 472, when he openly aligned himself with Themistocles and his policies by producing Aeschylus's play *The Persians*.[16] In the final part of his *Gorgias* in

13. Socrates was interested in the tendance of the soul, not the study of the physical world. See, for example, the *Apology* as a whole and his statement at 19c5–8: "I don't despise such knowledge [of physical and celestial phenomena] if anyone knows these things, but they do not interest me."

14. Plutarch reports (*Pericles* 36) that the older son, Xanthippus, was a spendthrift who publicly criticized his father. The accuracy of this is open to question.

15. See *Gorgias* 455e; *Theages* 126a9–10.

16. See above, pp. 15, 59–60.

particular, Plato makes Pericles, Cimon, Miltiades, and Themistocles emblematic of the greatest leaders that Athens had produced (503c2, 515d–519b and following) to pursue the argument that even the best politicians pander to the people, their master, and give them goods. They are demagogues, Socrates argues, who promote themselves; they do not promote the goodness of the people.[17]

The main interlocutors in this part of the dialogue are Callicles and Socrates.[18] Callicles, who admires political power, claims that the former Athenian leaders Themistocles, Cimon, Miltiades, and Pericles did much good for the citizens and are certainly better than the current leaders (503b3–c6):

> CALL.: But, by Zeus, I can name to you none of the present speakers in the assembly [who aim to improve the citizens].
>
> SOC.: Well, can you name any of the former leaders on whose account the Athenians became better when they were worse before? I myself do not know one such.

17. This charge of demagoguery against the democratic leaders, also found in the writers of Old Comedy, was reiterated by Plutarch and was one of the dominant ways of looking at the radical democracy of the Athenians up until relatively recent times. See J. T. Roberts, *Athens on Trial* (Princeton, 1994). Indeed, aristocrats often distrust the ability of ordinary people to govern: "[John Quincy] Adams believed that ordinary Americans weren't fit to govern themselves, that left to their own ignorance they would choose military heroes and demagogues who told them what they wanted to hear while leading them where they had no business going" (H. W. Brands, *Andrew Jackson: His Life and Times* [New York, 2005] 553).

18. Callicles is one of the few speakers in Plato who is otherwise completely unknown.

CALL.: What?! Have you not heard that Themistocles was a good man, and Cimon and Miltiades and the recently departed Pericles, whom you personally heard speak?

SOC.: Yes [they were good leaders], if, Callicles, what you said about virtue before is true, namely, that it is to satisfy completely one's own desires and those of others.

Pericles and other important leaders are also the focus of the following excerpts from the close of the *Gorgias* (515e–519d):

SOC.: Tell me this. Are the Athenians said to have become better because of Pericles or quite the opposite to have been destroyed by him? For I hear this very claim that Pericles by giving them pay made the Athenians lazy and worthless, empty talkers and money grubbers.

CALL.: You hear this, Socrates, from those whose ears don't function properly.

SOC.: These things are not hearsay, but I know them clearly, and so do you, namely, that Pericles at first had an unblemished reputation, and the Athenians, when they were inferior, found him guilty of no disgraceful wrongdoing. But when they had under his tutelage become beautiful and good, at the close of his life, they found him guilty of theft and nearly put him to death, clearly on the grounds that he was a knave. (515e2–516a3)

SOC.: Pericles had charge of the citizens, did he not?

CALL.: Of course.

SOC.: Well, was it not necessary, as we have just now been agreeing, that they become more just and not more unjust under his management, if indeed as one astute at politics he had care of them?

CALL.: Of course.

SOC.:   And just men are gentle as Homer says, are they not?

CALL.:   Yes.

SOC.:   But truly he produced citizens who were more unruly than the ones he received, and this came back to harm him, which he certainly didn't want.

CALL.:   Shall I agree?

SOC.:   Only if I seem to you to speak the truth.

CALL.:   Let it be so.

SOC.:   Then, if more unruly, they were also more unjust and more inferior, were they not?

CALL.:   Okay.

SOC.:   Then from this line of reasoning Pericles was not astute at politics.

CALL.:   If you say so. (516b8–d4)

Through this process of dialectic, Socrates brings the unwilling Callicles to the logical conclusion that Pericles was not a good leader. Socrates then continues in a similar vein about the great former leaders, and indeed all orators and politicians who only in the end care about their own advancement. Their claim to benefit their city and fellow citizens is hollow.

SOC.:   My dear man, I don't criticize them [Themistocles, Miltiades, Cimon, Pericles] that they were, you might say, stewards of the city; indeed, they seem to me to have been more serviceable than the men now, and they were more able to provide the city what it desired. As to transforming those desires and not giving in to them, but rather persuading and forcing their fellow citizens to that which would make them better, they differed not all from the current leaders. And yet, to become better is the sole task of a good citizen. I do, however, agree with you that they were more clever than the present group at providing ships and walls and dockyards and other such paraphernalia. (517b2–c3) . . .

You [Callicles] praise to the skies leaders who sumptuously entertained the citizens by indulging their every desire. And people say they made the city great. But they fail to realize that the city is bloated and has a festering wound because of them, these leaders of yore. Without moderation and justice they filled the city with harbors and dockyards and walls and money and other nonsense. Then, whenever the onset of the disease overtakes the citizens, they will blame their current advisers; but they will sing the praises of Themistocles, Cimon, and Pericles, those really responsible for their ills. And, if you are not careful, the citizens when they lose their original possessions in addition to what they have gained recently may attack you and my companion Alcibiades, although you are not the cause, but perhaps you do have some complicity.

And yet I now see and hear a senseless thing happening concerning these leaders of old. For I perceive that whenever the city pursues any of the politicians for wrongdoing, they get angry and complain bitterly of their suffering. That they should be undone unjustly by the city when they have done so many good things for it, such is their sad refrain. But the whole thing is a lie. For no leader of a city could ever be unjustly destroyed by the very city that he leads. Now it appears we have the same situation with those who claim to be politicians as we have with those who pretend to be teachers of wisdom. For these teachers being smart in other respects do this senseless thing. While claiming that they teach goodness, they frequently accuse their students of wronging them and not paying them and showing no gratitude, even though the students have been treated well. What could be more illogical than this claim that men who have become good and just, men whose injustice has been removed by their teachers and replaced with a sense of fair play, would have the capacity to do wrong? That does seem senseless to you, my friend, does it not? (518e1–519d5)

Plato here depicts Socrates as lumping together the politicians and the false teachers of wisdom; all pretend to benefit their charges but in fact do the opposite. The orators and politicians in particular seek popularity by giving in to the people. For Plato, then, Pericles suffered from the failings endemic to all political leaders: he had not devoted his life to philosophy, to the pursuit of wisdom. Nevertheless, he did stand out among them as one of the best of a flawed breed.

Plutarch and the
Biographical Tradition

Biography was not a developed genre in the ancient world even in the late first and early second century A.D. when Plutarch flourished. Interest in important individuals probably always existed, but persons or groups, such as soldiers killed in battle, were surely first celebrated in a formal manner in eulogies at funerals. A few highlights from the biographical tradition that was probably available to Plutarch follow.

In the fifth century, Ion of Chios (ca. 450 B.C.) wrote gossipy sketches of famous Athenians he visited, and Stesimbrotos of Thasos (ca. 420 B.C.) wrote *On Themistocles, Thucydides* [the politician], *and Pericles,* which seems to have been a scathing account of the education and training of the Athenian leaders who, to Stesimbrotos's thinking, had violently suppressed his city when it attempted to secede from the Delian League around 465. The fourth-century historian Xenophon (ca. 350 B.C.) wrote a posthumous encomium of Agesilaus, king of Sparta, and the *Cyropaedia,* a quasi-historical account of the upbringing of Cyrus, the Great King of Persia (ca. 557–ca. 530 B.C.). Xenophon's chief purpose in the latter was to represent styles of military and political leadership through fictional instructional passages.

Aristotle (384–322 B.C.) was interested in human behavior, particularly as exemplified in political history, and encouraged his followers to compile historical and comparative descriptions of 158 states. Theophrastus, his student, described types of human behavior in his *Characters,* a collection of essays. The collection format rather than single studies continued to be the model for "lives" into the Roman period: another student of Aristotle, Aristoxenus of Tarentum (fl. ca. 330 B.C.), wrote on the lives of at least four philosophers; about 240 B.C. Antigonus of Karystos composed sensational lives of the philosophers of his time; and Sotion of Alexandria (ca. 185 B.C.) created a rather ambitious compilation of philosophers' lives in thirteen books.

The birth-to-death biography of individual political figures does not seem to have existed in ancient times. There were early monographs on Alexander the Great at the height of his career by Ptolemy I (ca. 320 B.C.), Cleitarchus of Alexandria (ca. 310 B.C.), and Aristobulus of Cassandria (ca. 300 B.C.), and Roman generals and statesmen of the late Republic and early Empire sometimes wrote about their own exploits. These works, however, had political rather than biographical aims. Cicero's poem on his own consulship and the emperor Augustus's *Res gestae* are the best-known of this genre. Nicolaus of Damascus, friend of Herod the Great, inspired by the *Cyropaedia* of Xenophon, wrote on Augustus's life and education about 25 B.C. About the same time, the Roman writer Cornelius Nepos published his *On*

Illustrious Men in several books. Suetonius wrote *The Lives of the Twelve Caesars,* which was probably published somewhat later than Plutarch's *Lives.* Unlike Plutarch, he does not appear to have been interested in drawing moral lessons for his readers to emulate; rather, his main aim appears to have been to entertain, even titillate, his audience.

The range of these works is striking, although none is biography in the modern sense (i.e., the life of a single person told in detail). Praise (or, more rarely, blame) is the main purpose of these accounts, and all sought an audience—that is, their authors aspired to produce best sellers.

Plutarch's *Lives* is the most extensive example of ancient biography, presenting pairs of lives of important Greek and Roman political and military figures whom Plutarch considered similar. Plutarch exercised considerable influence in the imperial circle at Rome and used his writing to promote cooperation between Greece and Rome. His *Lives* are meant to instruct readers by illustrating individual virtues (or their opposite) as evidenced in the careers of eminent men. As he explains,

> virtue, by the bare statement of its actions, can so affect men's minds as to create at once both admiration of the things done and desire to imitate the doers of them. The goods of fortune we would possess and would enjoy; those of virtue we long to practise and exercise: we are content to receive the former from others, the latter we wish others to experience from us. Moral good is a practical stimulus; it is no sooner seen, than it inspires an impulse to practice, and influences the mind and character not by a mere imitation which we look at, but by the statement of the fact creates a moral purpose which we form. (Preface to *Lives of Pericles and Fabius Maximus,* sec. 2; trans. Dryden)

Plutarch explicitly states that his readers will be inspired to emulate the virtues of great men.[1] Chief among the virtues that made Pericles and Fabius Maximus most useful, according to Plutarch, were their gentle patience, innate sense of rightness, and unusual ability to put up with the follies of their fellow citizens and colleagues in government.

In large measure, then, Plutarch had ethical and pedagogical goals in mind and was not trying to write a balanced account of his subjects' lives and most important deeds. In fact, the ancients in general believed that a man's character is revealed by his deeds—or, as we might put it today, that "actions speak louder than words." Plutarch and others also felt that actions in small, everyday matters often revealed more about a man than his public deeds. Thus Plutarch's *Lives* often relate minor anecdotes rather than great affairs of state or momentous military feats.

Plutarch was born at Chaeronea in Boeotia before A.D. 50 and died fairly early in the reign of Hadrian (A.D. 117–138). Although he spent much of his life in his birthplace, he traveled widely, visited Egypt and Italy, lectured in Rome, and was granted citizenship in both Rome and Athens. He was a follower of Plato and had many important Roman friends including perhaps Trajan himself. For the last three decades or so of his life he served as a priest at Delphi and played a significant part in Delphi's revival as a religious center under Trajan and Hadrian.

---

1. See T. Duff, *Plutarch's Lives* (Oxford, 1999) 34–39, for a discussion of this passage, and more generally section 1 (pp. 13–98), which is entitled "The Moralizing Programme."

Plutarch was a prolific writer: seventy-five of his miscellaneous works survive in addition to the fifty *Lives*. The *Lives* are Plutarch's most enduring achievement, and though their value as source material challenges modern historians seeking true accounts, from the Renaissance to the present they have been a major source of information about important personages of the ancient world. Shakespeare knew the *Lives* in Thomas North's translation (1579) and made extensive use of them in writing his plays *Julius Caesar, Antony and Cleopatra,* and *Coriolanus*.

Plutarch composed his *Life of Pericles* about A.D. 100, approximately 530 years after Pericles' death; it is the first treatment of his life that we have. (See the appendix for the full text of the *Life* in Dryden's translation.) The *Life* has no clear structure but is arranged partly chronologically and partly thematically. It falls roughly into four parts: sections 1–6 present an introduction, followed by Pericles' lineage and education; 7–16 recount his political career; 17–37 describe his military leadership; and 38–39 give an account of his death and provide a summation of his greatness. Although Plutarch was about as remote in time from Pericles as we are from Christopher Columbus, he clearly had access to sources, both ancient writings and inscriptions, as well as architecture and art, that are no longer available to us. His quotation of the comic poets is especially valuable, as the foregoing discussion attests.

The major problem Plutarch's readers face is determining to what extent he can be trusted and to what extent the accounts he used were already contaminated by untrustworthy gossip and anecdote. As already noted, that difficulty is compounded by

Pericles' having become, like Alexander the Great, larger than life already in his own lifetime. Stories about him abounded, making it difficult to separate fact from fiction. In addition, Plutarch was quite willing to change certain facts to suit his pedagogical goals. It was fitting, for example, that the great democratic leader Pericles be a direct descendant of Cleisthenes, the so-called founder of the Athenian democracy, and Plutarch (*Pericles* 3.1) makes it so, even though he had intimate knowledge of the text of Herodotus where it is plainly stated (6.131) that Pericles was not, as Plutarch has it, the great-grandson, but rather the grandnephew of Cleisthenes on his mother's side. This is disturbing. How much else might Plutarch have altered that we can never recover?

While Plutarch's *Life of Pericles* must be read with caution, it includes a richness of detail that is of considerable interest. Plutarch "has furnished us with details not to be found elsewhere, and the anecdotes, even the scandalous gossip, which he reports, give us a glimpse of the world in which Pericles moved."[2] More important, he provides in a few cases entirely new information. Section 17, for example, constitutes our only source for the so-called Congress Decree through which Pericles allegedly sought to convene in Athens a meeting of all the Greeks to discuss the rebuilding of the temples destroyed by the Persians and the safe navigation of the sea. It was, however, completely predictable that the other Greeks would not participate and thus explicitly acknowledge the hegemony of Athens. Thus it is hard to credit Plutarch's claim that Pericles proposed and the Athenians enacted this measure, and even more so when he concludes his account as follows:

2. H. A. Holden, *Plutarch's Life of Pericles* (London, 1894) xxx.

Nothing was effected. . . . I thought fit, however, to introduce the mention of it, to show the spirit of the man and the greatness of his thoughts.

Pericles may have considered such a move, but it is hard to believe that he actually carried it through. At 20.1–2 Plutarch recounts in detail an expedition Pericles led to the Black Sea. He is our sole source for this.

More often, Plutarch offers information that supplements events already known to us. Among the most important is his account of the attacks of opponents of the building program, who accused Pericles of adorning Athens at the expense of the allies as though she were a wanton woman (12–13). He also gives us an intriguing account of Aspasia (24) in the context of the accusation against Pericles that it was she who had asked him to make war against Samos, to help out her native city of Miletus. His description of the conflict with Samos (25–28) fills out, though it largely agrees with and derives from, Thucydides' account (1.115–117). His interesting treatments of the Megarian decree (30), the attacks upon Pericles and his associates (31–32), and the opening campaigns of the war (33–35) clearly owe a great deal to his reading of Aristophanes and Thucydides.

Afterword

The Legend of Pericles

Except for Plutarch the authors discussed all lived at the same time as Pericles, or within a generation of his death. Many were his coevals and in a position either to have been personally acquainted with him or to have known people who were. Some, such as Anaxagoras, Protagoras, and Sophocles, were probably his good friends. The historian Thucydides too doubtless knew him personally and saw him on the street and in the assembly, but, inasmuch as he was at least thirty years younger than Pericles, it is doubtful that Pericles had any close association with him. Very few of these authors, however, wrote during Pericles' lifetime. The comic poets Cratinus and Telecleides certainly did so and expected that Pericles would hear their works. Herodotus too in my judgment composed much of his work prior to Pericles' death and might have expected that Pericles would be aware of what he wrote.[1]

---

1. See above, p. 109, n. 1. Some authors apparently gave public readings of their works.

Protagoras was probably reminiscing about Pericles soon after his death. Sophocles too, if he means us to think of Pericles when we read *Oedipus the King,* is writing about him posthumously and not long after 429 B.C. Although Lysias was born about 450 B.C., his activity as a speechwriter belongs to the early fourth century, well after Pericles' death.

The case of Thucydides is complicated. Although he began writing at the start of the war, as he himself tells us in the opening sentence of his *History* (1.1.1), much of his work as it has come down to us was demonstrably put in its final form when the war was over, that is, after 404 B.C., twenty-five years or more after Pericles died. The portrait that Thucydides gives us, the most extensive one we have, is thus at least in part the product of hindsight. He may be forgiven, therefore, if he has idealized Pericles somewhat, especially in the long view afforded by the ultimate defeat that Athens suffered in 404. In that light, Pericles' leadership at the beginning of the war may have looked particularly good.

Pericles was attacked during his lifetime, especially by the comic poets, and sometimes rather brutally (above, pp. 104–6). His fellow citizens actually fined him for his leadership of the war (Thucydides 2.65.3–4). Some who did not dare to attack him directly went after his friends. Phidias, the chief sculptor working on the Parthenon, for example, was clearly one of those attacked.[2] This has often been the way—get at the big man through his friends. Some conservative types criticized sharply Pericles' introduction of pay for jurors[3] and his building

2. Aristophanes *Peace* 600 ff. (above, p. 101).

3. Aristophanes *Wasps* 1117–1121 (above, p. 103); Plato *Gorgias* 515e5–7 (above, p. 139); also Aristotle *The Constitution of the Athenians* 27.4–5.

program.[4] There were also persistent rumors that he had bribed the Spartan king Pleistoanax to withdraw his troops from Attica in 446.[5] In short, Pericles faced a lot of opposition, some of it vehement.

There were surely those who hated him or, at the least, were jealous of his power. A number of his peers from the better families, the landed aristocracy, no doubt saw him as a traitor to his social class. They probably looked down on him as a demagogue, someone willing to sell out his birthright for political power. He certainly deserved some of the ill feeling, for there is no question that he could be ruthless in reducing his political adversaries to impotence. He used ostracism, for example, very effectively to remove opponents. Later in his career, when he was without question the leading man in the city, he was remote and either behaved in a somewhat imperious manner or appeared to many to do so. At the start of the war, he was heavily criticized for causing it (above, pp. 97–102). It was certainly said in some quarters that war could easily have been avoided if he had just been willing to give in a bit. It need not have happened, so they undoubtedly claimed. He had, some clearly felt, a private agenda. He was also attacked harshly for not leading Athenian troops into battle with the Spartans, but instead allowing them to lay waste Attica (above, pp. 65–68).

4. Plutarch (*Pericles* 12.1–2) mentions critics who attacked Pericles in the assembly for adorning Athens like a whore.

5. This was the famous occasion upon which Pericles replied, when asked what he had used the money for, "for what was necessary." Passages in Thucydides (2.21.1, 5.16.3) suggest that he did bribe the Spartan king. See also above, p. 18 n.7.

In practical terms, Pericles received the highest praise a man can receive from his fellow citizens when they reelected him year after year to the life-and-death post of general.[6] He was also chosen to speak over the city's fallen in two major conflicts, the Samian revolt and the initial campaigns of the Peloponnesian War (above, pp. 29–30, 68)—an honor that showed clear recognition of his preeminent reputation among his fellow citizens.

Most truly great men quickly become figures of legend; they take on larger-than-life dimensions. Soon after his death and even while he was alive, an aura of greatness surrounded Pericles. His reputation certainly grew exponentially as a result of his untimely death from the plague. Other leaders did not, perhaps could not, measure up. Even so, his growing reputation did not prevent the comic poets, at least in the first years after his death, from making posthumous attacks on him (above, p. 107). It is clear, however, that the historian Thucydides' presentation of him as a leader of Themistoclean stature (above, pp. 58–60), who, had he only lived, would have led his city to victory, very quickly came to predominate. The shrill voices of his harshest critics soon faded away and were largely forgotten. We have only an inkling of their accusations, mostly from the comic poets. The literary figures of the next generations consistently recognize Pericles as one of the greatest leaders of the city.[7] He quickly becomes canonically great, wise, and incorruptible. And the influence of Thucydides' portrait in creating that image is evident in later writers.

6. According to Plutarch (*Pericles* 16.3), it appears with more accuracy than exaggeration he was elected general for fifteen consecutive years after the ostracism of Thucydides son of Melesias in 443.

7. In his own sardonic way even Plato recognizes Pericles' preeminence.

Isocrates was born in 436 but became prominent as a teacher of rhetoric only in the fourth century. In his oration *Antidosis* (234–235), after naming Solon, Cleisthenes, and Themistocles, he continues:

> Lastly Pericles, who was a good leader of the people and the best speaker, so adorned the city that even now those visiting it believe the city not only worthy to rule the Hellenes, but all others as well; and, in addition to these things, he stored up on the Acropolis not less than 10,000 talents.

The *Antidosis* dates to the mid-fourth century B.C., to the year 353, to be precise; Isocrates wrote it when he was eighty-three. By this time, the inclusion of Pericles in the pantheon of democratic leaders had clearly become all but obligatory. In Isocrates' speech *On the Chariots* (28), the son of Alcibiades, Alcibiades the Younger, says about his father: "He was brought up by Pericles as guardian, a man whom everyone would agree was the most moderate, most just, and wisest of citizens."

About 330 B.C. Aristotle, or a member of his school, observed in *The Constitution of the Athenians:* "While Pericles was in charge of the people, the affairs of government were quite good; when he died, they became worse" (28.1; above, p. 22). The influence of Thucydides' final tribute to Pericles (2.65.5–13; above, pp. 88–90) on this statement about the decay in leadership after his demise is clear.

In the 330s, just a century after Pericles' death, Lycurgus, the leader of Athens, contrasts the simple honors awarded to Pericles for his great service with the elaborate ones requested for Demades, one of Lycurgus's political rivals, for relatively trivial accomplishments: "Pericles, the man who took Samos, Euboea, and Aegina,[8] the man who constructed the Propylaea, the Odeum,[9] and the Hecatompedon,[10] the man who stored up 10,000 talents of silver on the Acropolis, was crowned merely with an olive crown."[11] Of course, he did not do all of these things or, indeed, any of them, by himself. He had the considerable help of his fellow citizens. His name by metonymy stands for them all. Within a century of his death he has become the exemplar of the greatness of Athens in its heyday and remains so to the present day. The golden age of Athens is referred to as "Periclean Athens" or "Athens in the age of Pericles."

8. Aegina was seized and its citizens driven out in the summer of 431 (Thucydides 2.27.1–2). Although there is no evidence that Pericles was personally involved, this was done under his leadership, and Lycurgus is correct to give him the credit.

9. The Odeum is a large square building adjacent to the Theater of Dionysus in Athens. Its major use was apparently as a site for musical performances, and it is usually attributed to Pericles.

10. Hecatompedon is another name for the Parthenon.

11. *Against Demades* frag. 2 in *Minor Attic Orators,* vol. 2, ed. J. O. Burtt, Loeb Classical Library (Cambridge, Mass., 1954). Note that the canonical figure of 10,000 talents stored on the Acropolis, mentioned by both Isocrates and Lycurgus, almost certainly derives from rounding up the figure of 9,700 that Thucydides credits him with claiming in 2.13 (above, p. 62).

THE DRYDEN TRANSLATION
OF PLUTARCH'S *LIFE OF PERICLES*

The 1885 Dryden translation as revised by the Greek scholar A. H. Clough

(1) Caesar once seeing some wealthy strangers at Rome, carrying up and down with them in their arms and bosoms young puppy-dogs and monkeys, embracing and making much of them, took occasion not unnaturally to ask whether the women in their country were not used to bear children; by that prince-like reprimand gravely reflecting upon persons who spend and lavish upon brute beasts that affection and kindness which nature has implanted in us to be bestowed on those of our own kind. With like reason may we blame those who misuse that love of inquiry and observation which nature has implanted

Students may also wish to consult Ian Scott-Kilvert's translation of the *Life of Pericles* in *The Rise and Fall of Athens* (London, 1960) or Robin Waterfield's translation in *Plutarch, Greek Lives* (Oxford, 1998). For a commentary on the former, see A. J. Podlecki, *Plutarch, Life of Pericles* (Bristol, 1987).

By "Caesar," Plutarch means the emperor Augustus, who ruled the Roman world from 31 B.C. to 14 A.D.

in our souls, by expending it on objects unworthy of the attention either of their eyes or their ears, while they disregard such as are excellent in themselves, and would do them good. The mere outward sense, being passive in responding to the impression of the objects that come in its way and strike upon it, perhaps cannot help entertaining and taking notice of everything that addresses it, be it what it will, useful or unuseful; but, in the exercise of his mental perception, every man, if he chooses, has a natural power to turn himself upon all occasions, and to change and shift with the greatest ease to what he shall himself judge desirable. So that it becomes a man's duty to pursue and make after the best and choicest of everything, that he may not only employ his contemplation, but may also be improved by it. For as that colour is more suitable to the eye whose freshness and pleasantness stimulates and strengthens the sight, so a man ought to apply his intellectual perception to such objects as, with the sense of delight, are apt to call it forth, and allure it to its own proper good and advantage. Such objects we find in the acts of virtue, which also produce in the minds of mere readers about them an emulation and eagerness that may lead them on to imitation. In other things there does not immediately follow upon the admiration and liking of the thing done any strong desire of doing the like. Nay, many times, on the very contrary, when we are pleased with the work, we slight and set little by the workman or artist himself, as for instance, in perfumes and purple dyes, we are taken with the things themselves well enough, but do not think dyers and perfumers otherwise than low and sordid people. It was not said amiss by Antisthenes, when people told him that one Ismenias was an excellent piper. "It may be so," said he, "but he is but a wretched human being, otherwise he would not have been an excellent piper." And King Philip, to the same purpose, told his son Alexander, who once at a merry-meeting played a piece of music charmingly and skilfully, "Are you not ashamed, son, to play so well?" For it is enough for a king or prince to find leisure sometimes to hear others sing, and he does the muses quite honour enough when he pleases to be but present, while others engage in such exercises and trials of skill. (2) He who busies himself in mean occupations produces, in the very pains he takes about things of little or no use, an evidence against himself of his negligence and indisposition to what is really good. Nor did any generous and ingenuous young man, at the sight of the statue of Jupiter at Pisa, ever desire to be a Phidias, or on seeing that of Juno at Argos, long to be a Polycletus, or feel induced by his pleasure in their poems to wish to be an Anacreon or Philetas or Archilochus. For it does not necessarily follow, that, if a piece of work please for its gracefulness, therefore he that wrought it deserves our admiration. Whence it is that neither do such things really profit or advantage the beholders, upon the sight of which no zeal arises for the imitation of them, nor any impulse or inclination, which may prompt any desire or endeavour of doing the like. But virtue, by the bare statement of its actions, can so affect men's minds as to create at once both admiration of the things done and desire to imitate the doers of them. The goods of fortune we would possess and would enjoy; those of virtue we long to practise and exercise: we are content to receive the former from others, the latter we wish others to experience from us. Moral good is a practical stimulus; it is no sooner seen, than it inspires an impulse to practice, and influences the mind and character not by a mere imitation which we look at, but by the statement of the fact creates a moral purpose which we form. And so we have thought fit to spend our time and pains in writing of the lives of famous persons; and have composed this tenth book upon that subject, containing the life of Pericles, and that of Fabius Maximus, who carried on the war against Hannibal, men alike, as in their other virtues and good parts, so especially in their mind and upright temper and demeanour, and in that capacity to bear the cross-grained humours of their fellow-citizens and colleagues in office, which made them both most useful and serviceable to the interests of their countries. Whether we take a right aim at our intended purpose, it is left to the reader to judge by what he shall here find.

(3) Pericles was of the tribe Acamantis, and the township Cholargus, of the noblest birth both on his father's and mother's side. Xanthippus, his father, who defeated the King of Persia's generals in the battle of

Mycale, took to wife Agariste, the grandchild of Clisthenes, who drove out the sons of Pisistratus, and nobly put an end to their tyrannical usurpation, and, moreover, made a body of laws, and settled a model of government admirably tempered and suited for the harmony and safety of the people. His mother, being near her time, fancied in a dream that she was brought to bed of a lion, and a few days after was delivered of Pericles, in other respects perfectly formed, only his head was somewhat longish and out of proportion. For which reason almost all the images and statues that were made of him have the head covered with a helmet, the workmen apparently being willing not to expose him. The poets of Athens called him Schinocephalos, or squill-head, from schinos, a squill, or sea-onion. One of the comic poets, Cratinus, in the *Chirons,* tells us that

> "Old Chronos once took queen Sedition to wife:
> Which two brought to life
> That tyrant far-famed,
> Whom the gods the supreme skull-compeller have named;"

and, in the Nemesis, addresses him—

> "Come, Jove, thou head of Gods."

And a second, Teleclides, says, that now, in embarrassment with political difficulties, he sits in the city—

> "Fainting underneath the load
> Of his own head: and now abroad
> From his huge gallery of a pate
> Sends forth trouble to the state."

And a third, Eupolis, in the comedy called the *Demi,* in a series of questions about each of the demagogues, whom he makes in the play to come up from hell, upon Pericles being named last, exclaims—

> "And here by way of summary, now we've done,
> Behold, in brief, the heads of all in one."

(4) The master that taught him music, most authors are agreed, was Damon (whose name, they say, ought to be pronounced with the

first syllable short). Though Aristotle tells us that he was thoroughly practised in all accomplishments of this kind by Pythoclides. Damon, it is not unlikely, being a sophist, out of policy sheltered himself under the profession of music to conceal from people in general his skill in other things, and under this pretence attended Pericles, the young athlete of politics, so to say, as his training-master in these exercises. Damon's lyre, however, did not prove altogether a successful blind; he was banished from the country by ostracism for ten years, as a dangerous intermeddler and a favourer of arbitrary power, and, by this means, gave the stage occasion to play upon him. As, for instance, Plato, the comic poet, introduces a character who questions him—

> ". . . Tell me, if you please,
> Since you're the Chiron who taught Pericles."

Pericles, also, was a hearer of Zeno, the Eleatic, who treated of natural philosophy in the same manner as Parmenides did, but had also perfected himself in an art of his own for refuting and silencing opponents in argument; as Timon of Phlius describes it—

> "Also the two-edged tongue of mighty Zeno, who,
> Say what one would, could argue it untrue."

But he that saw most of Pericles, and furnished him most especially with a weight and grandeur of sense, superior to all arts of popularity, and in general gave him his elevation and sublimity of purpose and of character, was Anaxagoras of Clazomenae; whom the men of those times called by the name of Nous, that is, mind, or intelligence, whether in admiration of the great and extraordinary gift he had displayed for the science of nature, or because that he was the first of the philosophers who did not refer the first ordering of the world to fortune or chance, nor to necessity or compulsion, but to a pure, unadulterated intelligence, which in all other existing mixed and compound things acts as a principle of discrimination, and of combination of like with like.

(5) For this man, Pericles entertained an extraordinary esteem and admiration, and filling himself with this lofty and, as they call it,

up-in-the-air sort of thought, derived hence not merely, as was natural, elevation of purpose and dignity of language, raised far above the base and dishonest buffooneries of mob eloquence, but, besides this, a composure of countenance, and a serenity and calmness in all his movements, which no occurrence whilst he was speaking could disturb, a sustained and even tone of voice, and various other advantages of a similar kind, which produced the greatest effect on his hearers. Once, after being reviled and ill-spoken of all day long in his own hearing by some vile and abandoned fellow in the open market-place, where he was engaged in the despatch of some urgent affair. He continued his business in perfect silence, and in the evening returned home composedly, the man still dogging him at the heels, and pelting him all the way with abuse and foul language; and stepping into his house, it being by this time dark, he ordered one of his servants to take a light, and to go along with the man and see him safe home. Ion, it is true, the dramatic poet, says that Pericles's manner in company was somewhat over-assuming and pompous; and that into his high-bearing there entered a good deal of slightingness and scorn of others; he reserves his commendation for Cimon's ease and pliancy and natural grace in society. Ion, however, who must needs make virtue, like a show of tragedies, include some comic scenes, we shall not altogether rely upon; Zeno used to bid those who called Pericles's gravity the affectation of a charlatan, to go and affect the like themselves; inasmuch as this mere counterfeiting might in time insensibly instil into them a real love and knowledge of those noble qualities.

(6) Nor were these the only advantages which Pericles derived from Anaxagoras's acquaintance; he seems also to have become, by his instructions, superior to that superstition with which an ignorant wonder at appearances, for example, in the heavens, possesses the minds of people unacquainted with their causes, eager for the supernatural, and excitable through an inexperience which the knowledge of natural causes removes, replacing wild and timid superstition by the good hope and assurance of an intelligent piety.

There is a story, that once Pericles had brought to him from a country farm of his a ram's head with one horn, and that Lampon, the diviner, upon seeing the horn grow strong and solid out of the midst of the forehead, gave it as his judgment, that, there being at that time two potent factions, parties, or interests in the city, the one of Thucydides and the other of Pericles, the government would come about to that one of them in whose ground or estate this token or indication of fate had shown itself. But that Anaxagoras, cleaving the skull in sunder, showed to the bystanders that the brain had not filled up its natural place, but being oblong, like an egg, had collected from all parts of the vessel which contained it in a point to that place from whence the root of the horn took its rise. And that, for that time, Anaxagoras was much admired for his explanation by those that were present; and Lampon no less a little while after, when Thucydides was overpowered, and the whole affairs of the state and government came into the hands of Pericles.

And yet, in my opinion, it is no absurdity to say that they were both in the right, both natural philosopher and diviner, one justly detecting the cause of this event, by which it was produced, the other the end for which it was designed. For it was the business of the one to find out and give an account of what it was made, and in what manner and by what means it grew as it did; and of the other to foretell to what end and purpose it was so made, and what it might mean or portend. Those who say that to find out the cause of a prodigy is in effect to destroy its supposed signification as such, do not take notice, that, at the same time, together with divine prodigies, they also do away with signs and signals of human art and concert, as, for instance, the clashings of quoits, firebeacons, and the shadows of sun-dials, every one of which has its cause, and by that cause and contrivance is a sign of something else. But these are subjects, perhaps, that would better befit another place.

(7) Pericles, while yet but a young man, stood in considerable apprehension of the people, as he was thought in face and figure to be very like the tyrant Pisistratus, and those of great age remarked upon the sweetness of his voice, and his volubility and rapidity in speaking, and were struck with amazement at the resemblance. Reflecting, too, that

he had a considerable estate, and was descended of a noble family, and had friends of great influence, he was fearful all this might bring him to be banished as a dangerous person, and for this reason meddled not at all with state affairs, but in military service showed himself of a brave and intrepid nature. But when Aristides was now dead, and Themistocles driven out, and Cimon was for the most part kept abroad by the expeditions he made in parts out of Greece, Pericles, seeing things in this posture, now advanced and took his side, not with the rich and few, but with the many and poor, contrary to his natural bent, which was far from democratical; but, most likely fearing he might fall under suspicion of aiming at arbitrary power, and seeing Cimon on the side of the aristocracy, and much beloved by the better and more distinguished people, he joined the party of the people, with a view at once both to secure himself and procure means against Cimon.

He immediately entered, also, on quite a new course of life and management of his time. For he was never seen to walk in any street but that which led to the market-place and council-hall, and he avoided invitations of friends to supper, and all friendly visiting and intercourse whatever; in all the time he had to do with the public, which was not a little, he was never known to have gone to any of his friends to a supper, except that once when his near kinsman Euryptolemus married, he remained present till the ceremony of the drink-offering, and then immediately rose from table and went his way. For these friendly meetings are very quick to defeat any assumed superiority, and in intimate familiarity an exterior of gravity is hard to maintain. Real excellence, indeed, is most recognized when most openly looked into; and in really good men, nothing which meets the eyes of external observers so truly deserves their admiration, as their daily common life does that of their nearer friends. Pericles, however, to avoid any feeling of commonness, or any satiety on the part of the people, presented himself at intervals only, not speaking to every business, nor at all times coming into the assembly, but, as Critolaus says, reserving himself, like the Salaminian galley, for great occasions, while matters of lesser importance were despatched by friends or other speakers under his direction. And of this number we are told Ephialtes made one, who broke the power of the council of Areopagus, giving the people, according to Plato's expression, so copious and so strong a draught of liberty, that growing wild and unruly, like an unmanageable horse, it, as the comic poets say—

> "—got beyond all keeping in,
> Champing at Euboea, and among the islands leaping in."

(8) The style of speaking most consonant to his form of life and the dignity of his views he found, so to say, in the tones of that instrument with which Anaxagoras had furnished him; of his teaching he continually availed himself, and deepened the colours of rhetoric with the dye of natural science. For having, in addition to his great natural genius, attained, by the study of nature, to use the words of the divine Plato, this height of intelligence, and this universal consummating power, and drawing hence whatever might be of advantage to him in the art of speaking, he showed himself far superior to all others. Upon which account, they say, he had his nickname given him; though some are of opinion he was named the Olympian from the public buildings with which he adorned the city; and others again, from his great power in public affairs, whether of war or peace. Nor is it unlikely that the confluence of many attributes may have conferred it on him. However, the comedies represented at the time, which, both in good earnest and in merriment, let fly many hard words at him, plainly show that he got that appellation especially from his speaking; they speak of his "thundering and lightning" when he harangued the people, and of his wielding a dreadful thunderbolt in his tongue.

A saying also of Thucydides, the son of Melesias, stands on record, spoken by him by way of pleasantry upon Pericles's dexterity. Thucydides was one of the noble and distinguished citizens, and had been his greatest opponent; and, when Archidamus, the King of the Lacedaemonians, asked him whether he or Pericles were the better wrestler, he made this answer: "When I," said he, "have thrown him and given him a fair fall, by persisting that he had no fall, he gets the better of me, and makes the bystanders, in spite of their own eyes, believe him."

The truth, however, is, that Pericles himself was very careful what and how he was to speak, insomuch that, whenever he went up to the hustings, he prayed the gods that no one word might unawares slip from him unsuitable to the matter and the occasion.

He has left nothing in writing behind him, except some decrees; and there are but very few of his sayings recorded; one, for example, is, that he said Aegina must, like a gathering in a man's eye, be removed from Piraeus; and another, that he said he saw already war moving on its way towards them out of Peloponnesus. Again, when on a time Sophocles, who was his fellow-commissioner in the generalship, was going on board with him, and praised the beauty of a youth they met with in the way to the ship, "Sophocles," said he, "a general ought not only to have clean hands but also clean eyes." And Stesimbrotus tells us that, in his encomium on those who fell in battle at Samos, he said they were become immortal, as the gods were. "For," said he, "we do not see them themselves, but only by the honours we pay them, and by the benefits they do us, attribute to them immortality; and the like attributes belong also to those that die in the service of their country."

(9) Since Thucydides describes the rule of Pericles as an aristocratical government, that went by the name of a democracy, but was, indeed, the supremacy of a single great man, while many others say, on the contrary, that by him the common people were first encouraged and led on to such evils as appropriations of subject territory, allowances for attending theatres, payments for performing public duties, and by these bad habits were, under the influence of his public measures, changed from a sober, thrifty people, that maintained themselves by their own labours, to lovers of expense, intemperance, and licence, let us examine the cause of this change by the actual matters of fact.

At the first, as has been said, when he set himself against Cimon's great authority, he did caress the people. Finding himself come short of his competitor in wealth and money, by which advantages the other was enabled to take care of the poor, inviting every day some one or other of the citizens that was in want to supper, and bestowing clothes on the aged people, and breaking down the hedges and enclosures of his grounds, that all that would might freely gather what fruit they pleased, Pericles, thus outdone in popular arts, by the advice of one Damonides of Oea, as Aristotle states, turned to the distribution of the public moneys; and in a short time having bought the people over, what with moneys allowed for shows and for service on juries, and what with other forms of pay and largess, he made use of them against the council of Areopagus of which he himself was no member, as having never been appointed by lot—either chief archon, or lawgiver, or king, or captain. For from of old these offices were conferred on persons by lot, and they who had acquitted themselves duly in the discharge of them were advanced to the court of Areopagus. And so Pericles, having secured his power in interest with the populace, directed the exertions of his party against this council with such success, that most of these causes and matters which had been used to be tried there were, by the agency of Ephialtes, removed from its cognisance; Cimon, also, was banished by ostracism as a favourer of the Lacedaemonians and a hater of the people, though in wealth and noble birth he was among the first, and had won several most glorious victories over the barbarians, and had filled the city with money and spoils of war; as is recorded in the history of his life. So vast an authority had Pericles obtained among the people.

(10) The ostracism was limited by law to ten years; but the Lacedaemonians, in the meantime, entering with a great army into the territory of Tanagra, and the Athenians going out against them, Cimon, coming from his banishment before his time was out, put himself in arms and array with those of his fellow-citizens that were of his own tribe, and desired by his deeds to wipe off the suspicion of his favouring the Lacedaemonians, by venturing his own person along with his countrymen. But Pericles's friends, gathering in a body, forced him to retire as a banished man. For which cause also Pericles seems to have exerted himself more in that than in any battle, and to have been conspicuous above all for his exposure of himself to danger. All Cimon's friends, also, to a man, fell together side by side, whom Pericles had accused with him of taking part with the Lacedaemonians. Defeated in this battle on their own frontiers, and expecting a new and perilous attack with return of spring,

the Athenians now felt regret and sorrow for the loss of Cimon, and repentance for their expulsion of him. Pericles, being sensible of their feelings, did not hesitate or delay to gratify it, and himself made the motion for recalling him home. He, upon his return, concluded a peace betwixt the two cities; for the Lacedaemonians entertained as kindly feelings towards him as they did the reverse towards Pericles and the other popular leaders.

Yet some there are who say that Pericles did not propose the order for Cimon's return till some private articles of agreement had been made between them, and this by means of Elpinice, Cimon's sister; that Cimon, namely, should go out to sea with a fleet of two hundred ships, and be commander-in-chief abroad, with a design to reduce the King of Persia's territories, and that Pericles should have the power at home.

This Elpinice, it was thought, had before this time procured some favour for her brother Cimon at Pericles's hands, and induced him to be more remiss and gentle in urging the charge when Cimon was tried for his life; for Pericles was one of the committee appointed by the commons to plead against him. And when Elpinice came and besought him in her brother's behalf, he answered, with a smile, "O Elpinice, you are too old a woman to undertake such business as this." But, when he appeared to impeach him, he stood up but once to speak, merely to acquit himself of his commission, and went out of court, having done Cimon the least prejudice of any of his accusers.

How, then, can one believe Idomeneus, who charges Pericles as if he had by treachery procured the murder of Ephialtes, the popular statesman, one who was his friend, and of his own party in all his political course, out of jealousy, forsooth, and envy of his great reputation? This historian, it seems, having raked up these stories, I know not whence, has befouled with them a man who, perchance, was not altogether free from fault or blame, but yet had a noble spirit, and a soul that was bent on honour; and where such qualities are, there can no such cruel and brutal passion find harbour or gain admittance. As to Ephialtes, the truth of the story, as Aristotle has told it, is this: that having made himself formidable to the oligarchical party, by being an uncompromising asserter of the people's rights in calling to account and prosecuting those who any way wronged them, his enemies, lying in wait for him, by the means of Aristodicus the Tanagraean, privately despatched him.

Cimon, while he was admiral, ended his days in the Isle of Cyprus. (11) And the aristocratical party, seeing that Pericles was already before this grown to be the greatest and foremost man of all the city, but nevertheless wishing there should be somebody set up against him, to blunt and turn the edge of his power, that it might not altogether prove a monarchy, put forward Thucydides of Alopece, a discreet person, and a near kinsman of Cimon's, to conduct the opposition against him; who, indeed, though less skilled in warlike affairs than Cimon was, yet was better versed in speaking and political business and keeping close guard in the city, and, engaging with Pericles on the hustings, in a short time brought the government to an equality of parties. For he would not suffer those who were called the honest and good (persons of worth and distinction) to be scattered up and down and mix themselves and be lost among the populace, as formerly, diminishing and obscuring their superiority amongst the masses; but taking them apart by themselves and uniting them in one body, by their combined weight he was able, as it were upon the balance, to make a counterpoise to the other party.

For, indeed, there was from the beginning a sort of concealed split, or seam, as it might be in a piece of iron, marking the different popular and aristocratical tendencies; but the open rivalry and contention of these two opponents made the gash deep, and severed the city into the two parties of the people and the few. And so Pericles, at that time, more than at any other, let loose the reins to the people, and made his policy subservient to their pleasure, contriving continually to have some great public show or solemnity, some banquet, or some procession or other in the town to please them, coaxing his countrymen like children with such delights and pleasures as were not, however, unedifying. Besides that every year he sent out threescore galleys, on board of which there were numbers of the citizens, who were in pay eight months, learning at the same time and practising the art of seamanship.

He sent, moreover, a thousand of them into the Chersonese as planters, to share the land among them by lot, and five hundred more into the isle of Naxos, and half that number to Andros, a thousand into Thrace to dwell among the Bisaltae, and others into Italy, when the city Sybaris, which now was called Thurii, was to be repeopled. And this he did to ease and discharge the city of an idle, and, by reason of their idleness, a busy meddling crowd of people; and at the same time to meet the necessities and restore the fortunes of the poor townsmen, and to intimidate, also, and check their allies from attempting any change, by posting such garrisons, as it were, in the midst of them.

(12) That which gave most pleasure and ornament to the city of Athens, and the greatest admiration and even astonishment to all strangers, and that which now is Greece's only evidence that the power she boasts of and her ancient wealth are no romance or idle story, was his construction of the public and sacred buildings. Yet this was that of all his actions in the government which his enemies most looked askance upon and cavilled at in the popular assemblies, crying out how that the commonwealth of Athens had lost its reputation and was ill-spoken of abroad for removing the common treasure of the Greeks from the isle of Delos into their own custody; and how that their fairest excuse for so doing, namely, that they took it away for fear the barbarians should seize it, and on purpose to secure it in a safe place, this Pericles had made unavailable, and how that "Greece cannot but resent it as an insufferable affront, and consider herself to be tyrannized over openly, when she sees the treasure, which was contributed by her upon a necessity for the war, wantonly lavished out by us upon our city, to gild her all over, and to adorn and set her forth, as it were some vain woman, hung round with precious stones and figures and temples, which cost a world of money."

Pericles, on the other hand, informed the people, that they were in no way obliged to give any account of those moneys to their allies, so long as they maintained their defence, and kept off the barbarians from attacking them; while in the meantime they did not so much as supply one horse or man or ship, but only found money for the service; "which money," said he, "is not theirs that give it, but theirs that receive it, if so be they perform the conditions upon which they receive it." And that it was good reason, that, now the city was sufficiently provided and stored with all things necessary for the war, they should convert the overplus of its wealth to such undertakings as would hereafter, when completed, give them eternal honour, and, for the present, while in process, freely supply all the inhabitants with plenty. With their variety of workmanship and of occasions for service, which summon all arts and trades and require all hands to be employed about them, they do actually put the whole city, in a manner, into state-pay; while at the same time she is both beautiful and maintained by herself. For as those who are of age and strength for war are provided for and maintained in the armaments abroad by their pay out of the public stock, so, it being his desire and design that the undisciplined mechanic multitude that stayed at home should not go without their share of public salaries, and yet should not have them given them for sitting still and doing nothing, to that end he thought fit to bring in among them, with the approbation of the people, these vast projects of buildings and designs of work, that would be of some continuance before they were finished, and would give employment to numerous arts, so that the part of the people that stayed at home might, no less than those that were at sea or in garrisons or on expeditions, have a fair and just occasion of receiving the benefit and having their share of the public moneys.

The materials were stone, brass, ivory, gold, ebony, cypresswood; and the arts or trades that wrought and fashioned them were smiths and carpenters, moulders, founders and braziers, stone-cutters, dyers, goldsmiths, ivory-workers, painters, embroiderers, turners; those again that conveyed them to the town for use, merchants and mariners and ship-masters by sea, and by land, cartwrights, cattle-breeders, wagoners, rope-makers, flax-workers, shoemakers and leather-dressers,

road-makers, miners. And every trade in the same nature, as a captain
in an army has his particular company of soldiers under him, had its
own hired company of journeymen and labourers belonging to it
banded together as in array, to be as it were the instrument and body
for the performance of the service. Thus, to say all in a word, the occasions and services of these public works distributed plenty through
every age and condition.

(13) As then grew the works up, no less stately in size than exquisite
in form, the workmen striving to outvie the material and the design
with the beauty of their workmanship, yet the most wonderful thing
of all was the rapidity of their execution.

Undertakings, any one of which singly might have required, they
thought, for their completion, several successions and ages of men,
were every one of them accomplished in the height and prime of one
man's political service. Although they say, too, that Zeuxis once, having heard Agatharchus the painter boast of despatching his work with
speed and ease, replied, "I take a long time." For ease and speed in doing a thing do not give the work lasting solidity or exactness of beauty;
the expenditure of time allowed to a man's pains beforehand for the
production of a thing is repaid by way of interest with a vital force for
the preservation when once produced. For which reason Pericles's
works are especially admired, as having been made quickly, to last
long. For every particular piece of his work was immediately, even at
that time, for its beauty and elegance, antique; and yet in its vigour
and freshness looks to this day as if it were just executed. There is a
sort of bloom of newness upon those works of his, preserving them
from the touch of time, as if they had some perennial spirit and undying vitality mingled in the composition of them.

Phidias had the oversight of all the works, and was surveyor-general,
though upon the various portions other great masters and workmen
were employed. For Callicrates and Ictinus built the Parthenon; the
chapel at Eleusis, where the mysteries were celebrated, was begun by
Coroebus, who erected the pillars that stand upon the floor or pavement,
and joined them to the architraves; and after his death Metagenes of

Xypete added the frieze and the upper line of columns; Xenocles of Cholargus roofed or arched the lantern on top of the temple of Castor and Pollux; and the long wall, which Socrates says he himself heard Pericles propose to the people, was undertaken by Callicrates. This work Cratinus ridicules, as long in finishing—

> " 'Tis long since Pericles, if words would do it,
> Talked up the wall; yet adds not one mite to it."

The Odeum, or music-room, which in its interior was full of seats and ranges of pillars, and outside had its roof made to slope and descend from one single point at the top, was constructed, we are told, in imitation of the King of Persia's Pavilion; this likewise by Pericles's order; which Cratinus again, in his comedy called the *Thracian Women,* made an occasion of raillery—

> "So, we see here,
> Jupiter Long-pate Pericles appear,
> Since ostracism time, he's laid aside his head,
> And wears the new Odeum in its stead."

Pericles, also eager for distinction, then first obtained the decree for a contest in musical skill to be held yearly at the Panathenaea, and he himself, being chosen judge, arranged the order and method in which the competitors should sing and play on the flute and on the harp. And both at that time, and at other times also, they sat in this music-room to see and hear all such trials of skill.

The propylaea, or entrances to the Acropolis, were finished in five years' time, Mnesicles being the principal architect. A strange accident happened in the course of building, which showed that the goddess was not averse to the work, but was aiding and co-operating to bring it to perfection. One of the artificers, the quickest and the handiest workman among them all, with a slip of his foot fell down from a great height, and lay in a miserable condition, the physicians having no hope of his recovery. When Pericles was in distress about this, Minerva appeared to him at night in a dream, and ordered a course of treatment, which he applied, and in a short time and with great ease cured the man. And upon this occasion it was that he set up a brass statue of Minerva, surnamed Health, in the citadel near the altar, which they say was there before. But it was Phidias who wrought the goddess's image in gold, and he has his name inscribed on the pedestal as the workman of it; and indeed the whole work in a manner was under his charge, and he had, as we have said already, the oversight over all the artists and workmen, through Pericles's friendship for him; and this, indeed, made him much envied, and his patron shamefully slandered with stories, as if Phidias were in the habit of receiving, for Pericles's use, freeborn women that came to see the works. The comic writers of the town, when they had got hold of this story, made much of it, and bespattered him with all the ribaldry they could invent, charging him falsely with the wife of Menippus, one who was his friend and served as lieutenant under him in the wars; and with the birds kept by Pyrilampes, an acquaintance of Pericles, who, they pretended, used to give presents of peacocks to Pericles's female friends. And how can one wonder at any number of strange assertions from men whose whole lives were devoted to mockery, and who were ready at any time to sacrifice the reputation of their superiors to vulgar envy and spite, as to some evil genius, when even Stesimbrotus the Thracian has dared to lay to the charge of Pericles a monstrous and fabulous piece of criminality with his son's wife? So very difficult a matter is it to trace and find out the truth of anything by history, when, on the one hand, those who afterwards write it find long periods of time intercepting their view, and, on the other hand, the contemporary records of any actions and lives, partly through envy and ill-will, partly through favour and flattery, pervert and distort truth.

(14) When the orators, who sided with Thucydides and his party, were at one time crying out, as their custom was, against Pericles, as one who squandered away the public money, and made havoc of the state revenues, he rose in the open assembly and put the question to the people, whether they thought that he had laid out much; and they saying, "Too much, a great deal," "Then," said he, "since it is so, let the cost not go to your account, but to mine; and let the inscription upon

the buildings stand in my name." When they heard him say thus, whether it were out of a surprise to see the greatness of his spirit or out of emulation of the glory of the works, they cried aloud, bidding him to spend on, and lay out what he thought fit from the public purse, and to spare no cost, till all were finished.

At length, coming to a final contest with Thucydides which of the two should ostracize the other out of the country, and having gone through this peril, he threw his antagonist out, and broke up the confederacy that had been organized against him.

(15) So that now all schism and division being at an end, and the city brought to evenness and unity, he got all Athens and all affairs that pertained to the Athenians into his own hands, their tributes, their armies, and their galleys, the islands, the sea, and their wide-extended power, partly over other Greeks and partly over barbarians, and all that empire, which they possessed, founded and fortified upon subject nations and royal friendships and alliance.

After this he was no longer the same man he had been before, nor as tame and gentle and familiar as formerly with the populace, so as readily to yield to their pleasures and to comply with the desires of the multitude, as a steersman shifts with the winds. Quitting that loose, remiss, and, in some cases, licentious court of the popular will, he turned those soft and flowery modulations to the austerity of aristocratical and regal rule; and employing this uprightly and undeviatingly for the country's best interests, he was able generally to lead the people along, with their own wills and consents, by persuading and showing them what was to be done; and sometimes, too, urging and pressing them forward extremely against their will, he made them, whether they would or no, yield submission to what was for their advantage. In which, to say the truth, he did but like a skilful physician, who, in a complicated and chronic disease, as he sees occasion, at one while allows his patient the moderate use of such things as please him, at another while gives him keen pains and drug to work the cure. For there arising and growing up, as was natural, all manner of distempered feelings among a people which had so vast a command and dominion, he alone, as a great master, knowing how to handle and deal fitly with each one of them, and, in an especial manner, making that use of hopes and fears, as his two chief rudders, with the one to check the career of their confidence at any time, with the other to raise them up and cheer them when under any discouragement, plainly showed by this, that rhetoric, or the art of speaking, is, in Plato's language, the government of the souls of men, and that her chief business is to address the affections and passions, which are as it were the strings and keys to the soul, and require a skilful and careful touch to be played on as they should be. The source of this predominance was not barely his power of language, but, as Thucydides assures us, the reputation of his life, and the confidence felt in his character; his manifest freedom from every kind of corruption, and superiority to all considerations of money. Notwithstanding he had made the city of Athens, which was great of itself, as great and rich as can be imagined, and though he were himself in power and interest more than equal to many kings and absolute rulers, who some of them also bequeathed by will their power to their children, he, for his part, did not make the patrimony his father left him greater than it was by one drachma.

(16) Thucydides, indeed, gives a plain statement of the greatness of his power; and the comic poets, in their spiteful manner, more than hint at it, styling his companions and friends the new Pisistratidae, and calling on him to abjure any intention of usurpation, as one whose eminence was too great to be any longer proportionable to and compatible with a democracy or popular government. And Teleclides says the Athenians had surrendered up to him—

> "The tribute of the cities, and with them, the cities too,
>   to do with them as he pleases, and undo;
> To build up, if he likes, stone walls around a town;
>   and again, if so he likes, to pull them down;
> Their treaties and alliances, power, empire, peace, and war,
>   their wealth and their success forever more."

Nor was all this the luck of some happy occasion; nor was it the mere bloom and grace of a policy that flourished for a season; but having for forty years together maintained the first place among statesmen such as Ephialtes and Leocrates and Myronides and Cimon and Tolmides and Thucydides were, after the defeat and banishment of Thucydides, for no less than fifteen years longer, in the exercise of one continuous unintermitted command in the office, to which he was annually re-elected, of General, he preserved his integrity unspotted; though otherwise he was not altogether idle or careless in looking after his pecuniary advantage; his paternal estate, which of right belonged to him, he so ordered that it might neither through negligence be wasted or lessened, nor yet, being so full of business as he was, cost him any great trouble or time with taking care of it; and put it into such a way of management as he thought to be the most easy for himself, and the most exact. All his yearly products and profits he sold together in a lump, and supplied his household needs afterwards by buying everything that he or his family wanted out of the market. Upon which account, his children, when they grew to age, were not well pleased with his management, and the women that lived with him were treated with little cost, and complained of his way of housekeeping, where everything was ordered and set down from day to day, and reduced to the greatest exactness; since there was not there, as is usual in a great family and a plentiful estate, anything to spare, or over and above; but all that went out or came in, all disbursements and all receipts, proceeded as it were by number and measure. His manager in all this was a single servant, Evangelus by name, a man either naturally gifted or instructed by Pericles so as to excel every one in this art of domestic economy.

All this, in truth, was very little in harmony with Anaxagoras's wisdom; if, indeed, it be true that he, by a kind of divine impulse and greatness of spirit, voluntarily quitted his house, and left his land to lie fallow and to be grazed by sheep like a common. But the life of a contemplative philosopher and that of an active statesman are, I presume, not the same thing; for the one merely employs, upon great and good objects of thought, an intelligence that requires no aid of instruments nor supply of any external materials; whereas the other, who tempers and applies his virtue to human uses, may have occasion for affluence, not as a matter of necessity, but as a noble thing; which was Pericles's case, who relieved numerous poor citizens.

However, there is a story that Anaxagoras himself, while Pericles was taken up with public affairs, lay neglected, and that, now being grown old, he wrapped himself up with a resolution to die for want of food; which being by chance brought to Pericles's ear, he was horror-struck, and instantly ran thither, and used all the arguments and entreaties he could to him, lamenting not so much Anaxagoras's condition as his own, should he lose such a counsellor as he had found him to be; and that, upon this, Anaxagoras unfolded his robe, and showing himself, made answer: "Pericles," said he, "even those who have occasion for a lamp supply it with oil."

(17) The Lacedaemonians beginning to show themselves troubled at the growth of the Athenian power, Pericles, on the other hand, to elevate the people's spirit yet more, and to raise them to the thought of great actions, proposed a decree, to summon all the Greeks in what, part soever, whether of Europe or Asia, every city, little as well as great, to send their deputies to Athens to a general assembly, or convention, there to consult and advise concerning the Greek temples which the barbarians had burnt down, and the sacrifices which were due from them upon vows they had made to their gods for the safety of Greece when they fought against the barbarians; and also concerning the navigation of the sea, that they might henceforward pass to and fro and trade securely and be at peace among themselves.

Upon this errand there were twenty men, of such as were above fifty years of age, sent by commission; five to summon the Ionians and Dorians in Asia, and the islanders as far as Lesbos and Rhodes; five to visit all the places in the Hellespont and Thrace, up to Byzantium; and other five besides these to go to Boeotia and Phocis and Peloponnesus, and from hence to pass through the Locrians over to the neighbouring continent as far as Acarnania and Ambracia; and the rest to take their course through Euboea to the Oetaeans and the Malian Gulf, and to the Achaeans of Phthiotis and the Thessalians; all of them to treat

with the people as they passed, and persuade them to come and take
their part in the debates for settling the peace and jointly regulating
the affairs of Greece.

Nothing was effected, nor did the cities meet by their deputies, as
was desired; the Lacedaemonians, as it is said, crossing the design un-
derhand, and the attempt being disappointed and baffled first in Peloponnesus. I thought fit, however, to introduce the mention of it, to
show the spirit of the man and the greatness of his thoughts.

(18) In his military conduct, he gained a great reputation for wari-
ness; he would not by his good-will engage in any fight which had
much uncertainty or hazard; he did not envy the glory of generals
whose rash adventures fortune favoured with brilliant success, however they were admired by others; nor did he think them worthy his
imitation, but always used to say to his citizens that, so far as lay in his
power, they should continue immortal, and live for ever. Seeing
Tolmides, the son of Tolmaeus, upon the confidence of his former successes, and flushed with the honour his military actions had procured
him, making preparations to attack the Boeotians in their own country when there was no likely opportunity, and that he had prevailed
with the bravest and most enterprising of the youth to enlist themselves as volunteers in the service, who besides his other force made up
a thousand, he endeavoured to withhold him and to advise him from
it in the public assembly, telling him in a memorable saying of his,
which still goes about, that, if he would not take Pericles's advice, yet
he would not do amiss to wait and be ruled by time, the wisest counsellor of all. This saying, at that time, was but slightly commended; but
within a few days after, when news was brought that Tolmides himself had been defeated and slain in battle near Coronea, and that many
brave citizens had fallen with him, it gained him great repute as well
as good-will among the people, for wisdom and for love of his countrymen.

(19) But of all his expeditions, that to the Chersonese gave most sat-
isfaction and pleasure, having proved the safety of the Greeks who inhabited there. For not only by carrying along with him a thousand

fresh citizens of Athens he gave new strength and vigour to the cities, but also by belting the neck of land, which joins the peninsula to the continent, with bulwarks and forts from sea to sea, he put a stop to the inroads of the Thracians, who lay all about the Chersonese, and closed the door against a continual and grievous war, with which that country had been long harassed, lying exposed to the encroachments and influx of barbarous neighbours, and groaning under the evils of a predatory population both upon and within its borders.

Nor was he less admired and talked of abroad for his sailing around the Peloponnesus, having set out from Pegae, or The Fountains, the port of Megara, with a hundred galleys. For he not only laid waste the sea-coast, as Tolmides had done before, but also, advancing far up into the mainland with the soldiers he had on board, by the terror of his appearance drove many within their walls; and at Nemea, with main force, routed and raised a trophy over the Sicyonians, who stood their ground and joined battle with him. And having taken on board a supply of soldiers into the galleys out of Achaia, then in league with Athens, he crossed with the fleet to the opposite continent, and, sailing along by the mouth of the river Achelous, overran Acarnania and shut up the Oeniadae within their city walls, and having ravaged and wasted their country, weighed anchor for home with the double advantage of having shown himself formidable to his enemies, and at the same time safe and energetic to his fellow citizens; for there was not so much as any chance miscarriage that happened, the whole voyage through, to those who were under his charge.

(20) Entering also the Euxine Sea with a large and finely equipped fleet, he obtained for the Greek cities any new arrangements they wanted, and entered into friendly relations with them; and to the barbarous nations, and kings and chiefs round about them, displayed the greatness of the power of the Athenians, their perfect ability and confidence to sail where-ever they had a mind, and to bring the whole sea under their control. He left the Sinopians thirteen ships of war, with soldiers under the command of Lamachus, to assist them against Timesileus the tyrant; and when he and his accomplices had been

thrown out, obtained a decree that six hundred of the Athenians that were willing should sail to Sinope and plant themselves there with the Sinopians, sharing among them the houses and land which the tyrant and his party had previously held.

But in other things he did not comply with the giddy impulses of the citizens, nor quit his own resolutions to follow their fancies, when, carried away with the thought of their strength and great success, they were eager to interfere again in Egypt, and to disturb the King of Persia's maritime dominions. Nay, there were a good many who were, even then, possessed with that unblest and inauspicious passion for Sicily, which afterward the orators of Alcibiades's party blew up into a flame. There were some also who dreamt of Tuscany and Carthage, and not without plausible reason in their present large dominion and prosperous course of their affairs.

(21) But Pericles curbed this passion for foreign conquest, and unsparingly pruned and cut down their ever busy fancies for a multitude of undertakings; and directed their power for the most part to securing and consolidating what they had already got, supposing it would be quite enough for them to do, if they could keep the Lacedaemonians in check; to whom he entertained all along a sense of opposition; which, as upon many other occasions, so he particularly showed by what he did in the time of the holy war. The Lacedaemonians, having gone with an army to Delphi, restored Apollo's temple, which the Phocians had got into their possession, to the Delphians; immediately after their departure, Pericles, with another army, came and restored the Phocians. And the Lacedaemonians, having engraven the record of their privilege of consulting the oracle before others, which the Delphians gave them, upon the forehead of the brazen wolf which stands there, he, also, having received from the Phocians the like privilege for the Athenians, had it cut upon the same wolf of brass on his right side.

(22) That he did well and wisely in thus restraining the exertions of the Athenians within the compass of Greece, the events themselves that happened afterward bore sufficient witness. For, in the first place, the Euboeans revolted, against whom he passed over with forces; and

then, immediately after, news came that the Megarians were turned their enemies; and a hostile army was upon the borders of Attica, under the conduct of Plistoanax, King of the Lacedaemonians. Wherefore Pericles came with his army back again in all haste out of Euboea, to meet the war which threatened at home; and did not venture to engage a numerous and brave army eager for battle; but perceiving that Plistoanax was a very young man, and governed himself mostly by the counsel and advice of Cleandrides, whom the ephors had sent with him, by reason of his youth, to be a kind of guardian and assistant to him, he privately made trial of this man's integrity, and, in a short time, having corrupted him with money, prevailed with him to withdraw the Peloponnesians out of Attica. When the army had retired and dispersed into their several states, the Lacedaemonians in anger fined their king in so large a sum of money, that, unable to pay it, he quitted Lacedaemon; while Cleandrides fled, and had sentence of death passed upon him in his absence. This was the father of Gylippus, who overpowered the Athenians in Sicily. And it seems that this covetousness was an hereditary disease transmitted from father to son; for Gylippus also afterwards was caught in foul practices, and expelled from Sparta for it. But this we have told at large in the account of Lysander.

(23) When Pericles, in giving up his accounts of this expedition, stated a disbursement of ten talents, as laid out upon fit occasion, the people, without any question, nor troubling themselves to investigate the mystery, freely allowed of it. And some historians, in which number is Theophrastus the philosopher, have given it as a truth that Pericles every year used to send privately the sum of ten talents to Sparta, with which he complimented those in office, to keep off the war; not to purchase peace neither, but time, that he might prepare at leisure, and be the better able to carry on war hereafter.

Immediately after this, turning his forces against the revolters, and passing over into the island of Euboea with fifty sail of ships and five thousand men in arms, he reduced their cities, and drove out the citizens of the Chalcidians, called Hippobotae, horse-feeders, the chief persons for wealth and reputation among them; and removing all the Histiaeans out of the country, brought in a plantation of Athenians in their room; making them his one example of severity, because they had captured an Attic ship and killed all on board.

(24) After this, having made a truce between the Athenians and Lacedaemonians for thirty years, he ordered, by public decree, the expedition against the isle of Samos, on the ground, that, when they were bid to leave off their war with the Milesians they had not complied. And as these measures against the Samians are thought to have been taken to please Aspasia, this may be a fit point for inquiry about the woman, what art or charming faculty she had that enabled her to captivate, as she did, the greatest statesmen, and to give the philosophers occasion to speak so much about her, and that, too, not to her disparagement. That she was a Milesian by birth, the daughter of Axiochus, is a thing acknowledged. And they say it was in emulation of Thargelia, a courtesan of the old Ionian times, that she made her addresses to men of great power. Thargelia was a great beauty, extremely charming, and at the same time sagacious; she had numerous suitors among the Greeks, and brought all who had to do with her over to the Persian interest, and by their means, being men of the greatest power and station, sowed the seeds of the Median faction up and down in several cities. Aspasia, some say, was courted and caressed by Pericles upon account of her knowledge and skill in politics. Socrates himself would sometimes go to visit her, and some of his acquaintance with him; and those who frequented her company would carry their wives with them to listen to her. Her occupation was anything but creditable, her house being a home for young courtesans. Aeschines tells us, also, that Lysicles, a sheep-dealer, a man of low birth and character, by keeping Aspasia company after Pericles's death, came to be a chief man in Athens. And in Plato's *Menexenus,* though we do not take the introduction as quite serious, still thus much seems to be historical, that she had the repute of being resorted to by many of the Athenians for instruction in the art of speaking. Pericles's inclination for her seems, however, to have rather proceeded from the passion of love. He

had a wife that was near of kin to him, who had been married first to Hipponicus, by whom she had Callias, surnamed the Rich; and also she brought Pericles, while she lived with him, two sons, Xanthippus and Paralus. Afterwards, when they did not well agree, nor like to live together, he parted with her, with her own consent, to another man, and himself took Aspasia, and loved her with wonderful affection; every day, both as he went out and as he came in from the market-place, he saluted and kissed her.

In the comedies she goes by the nicknames of the new Omphale and Deianira, and again is styled Juno. Cratinus, in downright terms, calls her a harlot.

> "To find him a Juno the goddess of lust
> Bore that harlot past shame,
> Aspasia by name."

It should seem also that he had a son by her; Eupolis, in his *Demi,* introduced Pericles asking after his safety, and Myronides replying—

> "My son?" "He lives: a man he had been long,
> But that the harlot-mother did him wrong."

Aspasia, they say, became so celebrated and renowned, that Cyrus, also who made war against Artaxerxes for the Persian monarchy, gave her whom he loved the best of all his concubines the name of Aspasia, who before that was called Milto. She was a Phocaean by birth, the daughter of one Hermotimus, and, when Cyrus fell in battle, was carried to the king, and had great influence at court. These things coming into my memory as I am writing this story, it would be unnatural for me to omit them.

(25) Pericles, however, was particularly charged with having proposed to the assembly the war against the Samians, from favour to the Milesians, upon the entreaty of Aspasia. For the two states were at war for the possession of Priene; and the Samians, getting the better, refused to lay down their arms and to have the controversy betwixt them decided by arbitration before the Athenians. Pericles, therefore, fitting out a fleet, went and broke up the oligarchical government at Samos,

and taking fifty of the principal men of the town as hostages, and as many of their children, sent them to the isle of Lemnos, there to be kept, though he had offers, as some relate, of a talent apiece for himself from each one of the hostages, and of many other presents from those who were anxious not to have a democracy. Moreover, Pisuthnes the Persian, one of the king's lieutenants, bearing some good-will to the Samians, sent him ten thousand pieces of gold to excuse the city. Pericles, however, would receive none of all this; but after he had taken that course with the Samians which he thought fit, and set up a democracy among them, sailed back to Athens.

But they, however, immediately revolted, Pisuthnes having privily got away their hostages for them, and provided them with means for the war. Whereupon Pericles came out with a fleet a second time against them, and found them not idle nor slinking away, but manfully resolved to try for the dominion of the sea. The issue was, that after a sharp sea-fight about the island called Tragia, Pericles obtained a decisive victory, having with forty-four ships routed seventy of the enemy's, twenty of which were carrying soldiers.

(26) Together with his victory and pursuit, having made himself master of the port, he laid siege to the Samians, and blocked them up, who yet, one way or another, still ventured to make sallies, and fight under the city walls. But after that another greater fleet from Athens was arrived, and that the Samians were now shut up with a close leaguer on every side, Pericles, taking with him sixty galleys, sailed out into the main sea, with the intention, as most authors give the account, to meet a squadron of Phoenician ships that were coming for the Samians' relief, and to fight them at as great distance as could be from the island; but, as Stesimbrotus says, with a design of putting over to Cyprus, which does not seem to be probable. But, whichever of the two was his intention, it seems to have been a miscalculation. For on his departure, Melissus, the son of Ithagenes, a philosopher, being at that time the general in Samos, despising either the small number of the ships that were left or the inexperience of the commanders, prevailed with the citizens to attack the Athenians. And the Samians having won

the battle, and taken several of the men prisoners, and disabled several of the ships, were masters of the sea, and brought into port all necessaries they wanted for the war, which they had not before. Aristotle says, too, that Pericles had been once before this worsted by this Melissus in a sea-fight.

The Samians, that they might requite an affront which had before been put upon them, branded the Athenians, whom they took prisoners, in their foreheads, with the figure of an owl. For so the Athenians had marked them before with a Samaena, which is a sort of ship, low and flat in the prow, so as to look snub-nosed, but wide and large and well-spread in the hold, by which it both carries a large cargo and sails well. And it was so called, because the first of that kind was seen at Samos, having been built by order of Polycrates the tyrant. These brands upon the Samians' foreheads, they say, are the allusion in the passage of Aristophanes, where he says—

"For, oh, the Samians are a lettered people."

(27) Pericles, as soon as news was brought him of the disaster that had befallen his army, made all the haste he could to come in to their relief, and having defeated Melissus, who bore up against him, and put the enemy to flight, he immediately proceeded to hem them in with a wall, resolving to master them and take the town, rather with some cost and time than with the wounds and hazards of his citizens. But as it was a hard matter to keep back the Athenians, who were vexed at the delay, and were eagerly bent to fight, he divided the whole multitude into eight parts, and arranged by lot that that part which had the white bean should have leave to feast and take their ease while the other seven were fighting. And this is the reason, they say, that people, when at any time they have been merry, and enjoyed themselves, called it white day, in allusion to this white bean.

Ephorus the historian tells us besides, that Pericles made use of engines of battery in this siege, being much taken with the curiousness of the invention, with the aid and presence of Artemon himself, the engineer, who, being lame, used to be carried about in a litter, where the works required his attendance, and for that reason was called Pe-riphoretus. But Heraclides Ponticus disproves this out of Anacreon's poems, where mention is made of this Artemon Periphoretus several ages before the Samian war, or any of these occurrences. And he says that Artemon, being a man who loved his ease, and had a great appre-hension of danger, for the most part kept close within doors, having two of his servants to hold a brazen shield over his head, that nothing might fall upon him from above; and if he were at any time forced upon necessity to go abroad, that he was carried about in a little hang-ing bed, close to the very ground, and that for this reason he was called Periphoretus.

(28) In the ninth month, the Samians surrendering themselves and delivering up the town, Pericles pulled down their walls, and seized their shipping, and set a fine of a large sum of money upon them, part of which they paid down at once, and they agreed to bring in the rest by a certain time, and gave hostages for security. Duris the Samian makes a tragical drama out of these events, charging the Athenians and Pericles with a great deal of cruelty, which neither Thucydides, nor Ephorus, nor Aristotle have given any relation of, and probably with little regard to truth; how, for example, he brought the captains and soldiers of the galleys into the market-place at Miletus, and there having bound them fast to boards for ten days, then, when they were already all but half dead, gave order to have them killed by beating out their brains with clubs, and their dead bodies to be flung out into the open streets and fields, unburied. Duris however, who, even where he has no private feeling concerned, is not wont to keep his narratives within the limits of truth, is the more likely upon this occasion to have exaggerated the calamities which befell his country, to create odium against the Athenians. Pericles however, after the reduction of Samos, returning back to Athens, took care that those who died in the war should be honourably buried, and made a funeral harangue, as the custom is, in their commendation at their graves, for which he gained great admiration. As he came down from the stage on which he spoke, the rest of the women came and complimented him, taking him by the

hand, and crowning him with garlands and ribbons, like a victorious athlete in the games; but Elpinice, coming near to him, said, "These are brave deeds, Pericles, that you have done, and such as deserve our chaplets; who have lost us many a worthy citizen, not in a war with Phoenicians or Medes, like my brother Cimon, but for the overthrow of an allied and kindred city." As Elpinice spoke these words, he, smiling quietly, as it is said, returned her answer with this verse:—

"Old women should not seek to be perfumed."

Ion says of him, that upon this exploit of his, conquering the Samians, he indulged very high and proud thoughts of himself: whereas Agamemnon was ten years taking a barbarous city, he had in nine months' time vanquished and taken the greatest and most powerful of the Ionians. And indeed it was not without reason that he assumed this glory to himself, for, in real truth, there was much uncertainty and great hazard in this great war, if so be, as Thucydides tells us, the Samian state were within a very little of wresting the whole power and dominion of the sea out of the Athenians' hands.

(29) After this was over, the Peloponnesian war beginning to break out in full tide, he advised the people to send help to the Corcyraeans, who were attacked by the Corinthians, and to secure to themselves an island possessed of great naval resources, since the Peloponnesians were already all but in actual hostilities against them. The people readily consenting to the motion, and voting an aid and succour for them, he despatched Lacedaemonius, Cimon's son, having only ten ships with him, as it were out of a design to affront him; for there was a great kindness and friendship betwixt Cimon's family and the Lacedaemonians; so, in order that Lacedaemonius might lie the more open to a charge, or suspicion at least, of favouring the Lacedaemonians and playing false, if he performed no considerable exploit in this service, he allowed him a small number of ships, and sent him out against his will; and indeed he made it somewhat his business to hinder Cimon's sons from rising in the state, professing that by their very names they were not to be looked upon as native and true Athenians,

but foreigners and strangers, one being called Lacedaemonius, another Thessalus, and the third Eleus and they were all three of them, it was thought, born of an Arcadian woman. Being, however, ill spoken of on account of these ten galleys, as having afforded but a small supply to the people that were in need, and yet given a great advantage to those who might complain of the act of intervention, Pericles sent out a larger force afterwards to Corcyra, which arrived after the fight was over. And when now the Corinthians, angry and indignant with the Athenians, accused them publicly at Lacedaemon, the Megarians joined with them, complaining that they were, contrary to common right and the articles of peace sworn to among the Greeks, kept out and driven away from every market and from all ports under the control of the Athenians. The Aeginetans, also, professing to be ill-used and treated with violence, made supplications in private to the Lacedaemonians for redress, though not daring openly to call the Athenians in question. In the meantime, also, the city Potidaea, under the dominion of the Athenians, but a colony formerly of the Corinthians, had revolted, and was beset with a formal siege, and was a further occasion of precipitating the war.

Yet notwithstanding all this, there being embassies sent to Athens, and Archidamus, the King of the Lacedaemonians, endeavouring to bring the greater part of the complaints and matters in dispute to a fair determination, and to pacify and allay the hearts of the allies, it is very likely that the war would not upon any other grounds of quarrel have fallen upon the Athenians, could they have been prevailed with to repeal the ordinance against the Megarians, and to be reconciled to them. Upon which account, since Pericles was the man who mainly opposed it, and stirred up the people's passions to persist in their contention with the Megarians, he was regarded as the sole cause of the war.

(30) They say, moreover, that ambassadors went, by order, from Lacedaemon to Athens about this very business, and that when Pericles was urging a certain law which made it illegal to take down or withdraw the tablet of the decree, one of the ambassadors, Polyalces by

name, said, "Well, do not take it down then, but turn it; there is no law, I suppose, which forbids that;" which, though prettily said, did not move Pericles from his resolution. There may have been, in all likelihood, something of a secret grudge and private animosity which he had against the Megarians. Yet, upon a public and open charge against them, that they had appropriated part of the sacred land on the frontier, he proposed a decree that a herald should be sent to them, and the same also to the Lacedaemonians, with an accusation of the Megarians; an order which certainly shows equitable and friendly proceeding enough. And after that the herald who was sent, by name Anthemocritus, died, and it was believed that the Megarians had contrived his death, then Charinus proposed a decree against them, that there should be an irreconcilable and implacable enmity thenceforward betwixt the two commonwealths; and that if any one of the Megarians should but set his foot in Attica, he should be put to death; and that the commanders, when they take the usual oath, should, over and above that, swear that they will twice every year make an inroad into the Megarian country; and that Anthemocritus should be buried near the Thracian Gates, which are now called the Dipylon, or Double Gate. On the other hand, the Megarians, utterly denying and disowning the murder of Anthemocritus, throw the whole matter upon Aspasia and Pericles, availing themselves of the famous verses in the *Acharnians*—

> "To Megara some of our madcaps ran
> And stole Simaetha thence, their courtesan.
> Which exploit the Megarians to outdo,
> Came to Aspasia's house, and took off two."

(31) The true occasion of the quarrel is not so easy to find out. But of inducing the refusal to annul the decree, all alike charge Pericles. Some say he met the request with a positive refusal, out of high spirit and a view of the state's best interest, accounting that the demand made in those embassies was designed for a trial of their compliance, and that a concession would be taken for a confession of weakness as if they durst not do otherwise; while other some there are who say that it

was rather out of arrogance and a willful spirit of contention, to show his own strength, that he took occasion to slight the Lacedaemonians. The worst motive of all, which is confirmed by most witnesses, is to the following effect: Phidias the Moulder had, as has before been said, undertaken to make the statue of Minerva. Now he, being admitted to friendship with Pericles, and a great favourite of his, had many enemies upon this account, who envied and maligned him; who also, to make trial in a case of his, what kind of judges the commons would prove, should there be occasion to bring Pericles himself before them, having tampered with Menon, one who had been a workman with Phidias, stationed him in the market-place, with a petition desiring public security upon his discovery and impeachment of Phidias. The people admitting the man to tell his story, and the prosecution proceeding in the assembly, there was nothing of theft or cheat proved against him; for Phidias, from the very first beginning, by the advice of Pericles, had so wrought and wrapt the gold that was used in the work about the statue, that they might take it all off, and make out the just weight of it, which Pericles at that time bade the accuser do. But the reputation of his works was what brought envy upon Phidias, especially that where he represents the fight of the Amazons upon the goddess's shield, he had introduced a likeness of himself as a bald old man holding up a great stone with both hands, and had put in a very fine representation of Pericles fighting with an Amazon. And the position of the hand which holds out the spear in front of the face, was ingeniously contrived to conceal in some degree the likeness, which meantime showed itself on either side.

Phidias then was carried away to prison, and there died of a disease; but, as some say, of poison, administered by the enemies of Pericles, to raise a slander, or a suspicion at least, as though he had procured it. The informer Menon, upon Glycon's proposal, the people made free from payment of taxes and customs, and ordered the generals to take care that nobody should do him any hurt.

(32) About the same time, Aspasia was indicted of impiety, upon the complaint of Hermippus the comedian, who also laid further to

her charge that she received into her house freeborn women for the uses of Pericles. And Diopithes proposed a decree, that public accusations should be laid against persons who neglected religion, or taught new doctrines about things above, directing suspicion, by means of Anaxagoras, against Pericles himself. The people receiving and admitting these accusations and complaints, at length, by this means, they came to enact a decree, at the motion of Dracontides, that Pericles should bring in the accounts of the moneys he had expended, and lodge them with the Prytanes; and that the judges, carrying their suffrage from the altar in the Acropolis, should examine and determine the business in the city. This last clause Hagnon took out of the decree, and moved that the causes should be tried before fifteen hundred jurors, whether they should be styled prosecutions for robbery, or bribery, or any kind of malversation. Aspasia, Pericles begged off, shedding, as Aeschines says, many tears at the trial, and personally entreating the jurors. But fearing how it might go with Anaxagoras, he sent him out of the city. And finding that in Phidias's case he had miscarried with the people, being afraid of impeachment, he kindled the war, which hitherto had lingered and smothered, and blew it up into a flame; hoping, by that means, to disperse and scatter these complaints and charges, and to allay their jealousy; the city usually throwing herself upon him alone, and trusting to his sole conduct, upon the urgency of great affairs and public dangers, by reason of his authority and the sway he bore.

These are given out to have been the reasons which induced Pericles not to suffer the people of Athens to yield to the proposals of the Lacedaemonians; but their truth is uncertain.

(33) The Lacedaemonians, for their part, feeling sure that if they could once remove him, they might be at what terms they pleased with the Athenians, sent them word that they should expel the "Pollution" with which Pericles on the mother's side was tainted, as Thucydides tells us. But the issue proved quite contrary to what those who sent the message expected; instead of bringing Pericles under suspicion and reproach, they raised him into yet greater credit and esteem with the cit-

izens, as a man whom their enemies most hated and feared. In the same way, also, before Archidamus, who was at the head of the Peloponnesians, made his invasion into Attica, he told the Athenians beforehand, that if Archidamus, while he laid waste the rest of the country, should forbear and spare his estate, either on the ground of friendship or right of hospitality that was betwixt them, or on purpose to give his enemies an occasion of traducing him; that then he did freely bestow upon the state all his land and the buildings upon it for the public use. The Lacedaemonians, therefore, and their allies, with a great army, invaded the Athenian territories, under the conduct of King Archidamus, and laying waste the country, marched on as far as Acharnae, and there pitched their camp, presuming that the Athenians would never endure that, but would come out and fight them for their country's and their honour's sake. But Pericles looked upon it as dangerous to engage in battle, to the risk of the city itself, against sixty thousand men-at-arms of Peloponnesians and Boeotians; for so many they were in number that made the inroad at first; and he endeavoured to appease those who were desirous to fight, and were grieved and discontented to see how things went, and gave them good words, saying, that "trees, when they are lopped and cut, grow up again in a short time, but men, being once lost, cannot easily be recovered." He did not convene the people into an assembly, for fear lest they should force him to act against his judgment; but, like a skilful steersman or pilot of a ship, who, when a sudden squall comes on, out at sea, makes all his arrangements, sees that all is tight and fast, and then follows the dictates of his skill, and minds the business of the ship, taking no notice of the tears and entreaties of the sea-sick and fearful passengers, so he, having shut up the city gates, and placed guards at all posts for security, followed his own reason and judgment, little regarding those that cried out against him and were angry at his management, although there were a great many of his friends that urged him with requests, and many of his enemies threatened and accused him for doing as he did, and many made songs and lampoons upon him, which were sung about the town to his disgrace, reproaching him with the cowardly exercise of his office of general, and the tame abandonment of every-thing to the enemy's hands.

Cleon, also, already was among his assailants, making use of the feeling against him as a step to the leadership of the people, as appears inthe anapaestic verses of Hermippus—

> "Satyr-king, instead of swords,
> Will you always handle words?
> Very brave indeed we find them,
> But a Teles lurks behind them.

> "Yet to gnash your teeth you're seen,
> When the little dagger keen,
> Whetted every day anew,
> Of sharp Cleon touches you."

(34) Pericles, however, was not at all moved by any attacks, but took all patiently, and submitted in silence to the disgrace they threw upon him and the ill-will they bore him; and, sending out a fleet of a hundred galleys to Peloponnesus, he did not go along with it in per-son, but stayed behind, that he might watch at home and keep the city under his own control, till the Peloponnesians broke up their camp and were gone. Yet to soothe the common people, jaded and distressed with the war, he relieved them with distributions of public moneys, and ordained new divisions of subject land. For having turned out all the people of Aegina, he parted the island among the Athenians ac-cording to lot. Some comfort also, and ease in their miseries, they might receive from what their enemies endured. For the fleet, sailing round the Peloponnese, ravaged a great deal of the country, and pil-laged and plundered the towns and smaller cities; and by land he him-self entered with an army the Megarian country, and made havoc of it all. Whence it is clear that the Peloponnesians, though they did the Athenians much mischief by land, yet suffering as much themselves from them by sea, would not have protracted the war to such a length, but would quickly have given it over, as Pericles at first foretold they would, had not some divine power crossed human purposes.

In the first place, the pestilential disease, or plague, seized upon the city, and ate up all the flower and prime of their youth and strength. Upon occasion of which, the people, distempered and afflicted in their souls, as well as in their bodies, were utterly enraged like madmen against Pericles, and, like patients grown delirious, sought to lay violent hands on their physician, or, as it were, their father. They had been possessed, by his enemies, with the belief that the occasion of the plague was the crowding of the country people together into the town forced as they were now, in the heat of the summer-weather, to dwell many of them together even as they could, in small tenements and stifling hovels, and to be tied to a lazy course of life within doors, whereas before they lived in a pure, open, and free air. The cause and author of all this, said they, is he who on account of the war has poured a multitude of people in upon us within the walls, and uses all these men that he has here upon no employ or service, but keeps them pent up like cattle, to be overrun with infection from one another, affording them neither shift of quarters nor any refreshment.

(35) With the design to remedy these evils, and do the enemy some inconvenience, Pericles got a hundred and fifty galleys ready, and having embarked many tried soldiers, both foot and horse, was about to sail out, giving great hope to his citizens, and no less alarm to his enemies, upon the sight of so great a force. And now the vessels having their complement of men, and Pericles being gone aboard his own galley, it happened that the sun was eclipsed, and it grew dark on a sudden, to the affright of all, for this was looked upon as extremely ominous. Pericles, therefore, perceiving the steersman seized with fear and at a loss what to do, took his cloak and held it up before the man's face, and screening him with it so that he could not see, asked him whether he imagined there was any great hurt, or the sign of any great hurt in this, and he answering No, "Why," said he, "and what does that differ from this, only that what has caused that darkness there, is something greater than a cloak?" This is a story which philosophers tell their scholars. Pericles, however, after putting out to sea, seems not to have done any other exploit befitting such preparations, and when

he had laid siege to the holy city Epidaurus, which gave him some hope of surrender, miscarried in his design by reason of the sickness. For it not only seized upon the Athenians, but upon all others, too, that held any sort of communication with the army. Finding after this the Athenians ill-affected and highly displeased with him, he tried and endeavoured what he could to appease and re-encourage them. But he could not pacify or allay their anger, nor persuade or prevail with them any way, till they freely passed their votes upon him, resumed their power, took away his command from him, and fined him in a sum of money; which by their account that say least, was fifteen talents, while they who reckon most, name fifty. The name prefixed to the accusation was Cleon, as Idomeneus tells us; Simmias, according to Theophrastus; and Heraclides Ponticus gives it as Lacratidas.

(36) After this, public troubles were soon to leave him unmolested; the people, so to say, discharged their passion in their stroke, and lost their stings in the wound. But his domestic concerns were in an unhappy condition, many of his friends and acquaintance having died in the plague time, and those of his family having long since been in disorder and in a kind of mutiny against him. For the eldest of his lawfully begotten sons, Xanthippus by name, being naturally prodigal, and marrying a young and expensive wife, the daughter of Tisander, son of Epilycus, was highly offended at his father's economy in making him but a scanty allowance, by little and little at a time. He sent, therefore, to a friend one day and borrowed some money of him in his father Pericles's name, pretending it was by his order. The man coming afterward to demand the debt, Pericles was so far from yielding to pay it, that he entered an action against him. Upon which the young man, Xanthippus, thought himself so ill-used and disobliged that he openly reviled his father; telling first, by way of ridicule, stories about his conversations at home, and the discourses he had with the sophists and scholars that came to his house. As, for instance, how one who was a practicer of the five games of skill, having with a dart or javelin unawares against his will struck and killed Epitimus the Pharsalian, his father spent a whole day with Protagoras in a serious dispute, whether

the javelin, or the man that threw it, or the masters of the games who appointed these sports, were, according to the strictest and best reason, to be accounted the cause of this mischance. Besides this, Stesimbrotus tells us that it was Xanthippus who spread abroad among the people the infamous story concerning his own wife; and in general that this difference of the young man's with his father, and the breach betwixt them, continued never to be healed or made up till his death. For Xanthippus died in the plague time of the sickness. At which time Pericles also lost his sister, and the greatest part of his relations and friends, and those who had been most useful and serviceable to him in managing the affairs of state. However, he did not shrink or give in upon these occasions, nor betray or lower his high spirit and the greatness of his mind under all his misfortunes; he was not even so much as seen to weep or to mourn, or even attend the burial of any of his friends or relations, till at last he lost his only remaining legitimate son. Subdued by this blow, and yet striving still, as far as he could, to maintain his principle, and to preserve and keep up the greatness of his soul, when he came, however, to perform the ceremony of putting a garland of flowers upon the head of the corpse, he was vanquished by his passion at the sight, so that he burst into exclamations, and shed copious tears, having never done any such thing in his life before.

(37) The city having made trial of other generals for the conduct of war, and orators for business of state, when they found there was no one who was of weight enough for such a charge, or of authority sufficient to be trusted with so great a command regretted the loss of him, and invited him again to address and advise them, and to reassume the office of general. He, however, lay at home in dejection and mourning; but was persuaded by Alcibiades and others of his friends to come abroad and show himself to the people; who having, upon his appearance, made their acknowledgments, and apologized for their untowardly treatment of him he undertook the public affairs once more; and, being chosen general, requested that the statute concerning baseborn children, which he himself had formerly caused to be made, might be suspended; that so the name and race of his family might not,

for absolute want of a lawful heir to succeed, be wholly lost and extinguished. The case of the statute was thus: Pericles, when long ago at the height of his power in the state, having then, as has been said, children lawfully begotten, proposed a law that those only should be reputed true citizens of Athens who were born of such parents as were both Athenians. After this, the King of Egypt having sent to the people, by way of present, forty thousand bushels of wheat, which were to be shared out among the citizens, a great many actions and suits about legitimacy occurred, by virtue of that edict; cases which, till that time, had not been known nor taken notice of; and several persons suffered by false accusations. There were little less than five thousand who were convicted and sold for slaves; those who, enduring the test, remained in the government and passed muster for true Athenians were found upon the poll to be fourteen thousand and forty persons in number.

It looked strange, that a law, which had been carried so far against so many people, should be cancelled again by the same man that made it; yet the present calamity and distress which Pericles laboured under in his family broke through all objections, and prevailed with the Athenians to pity him, as one whose losses and misfortunes had sufficiently punished his former arrogance and haughtiness. His sufferings deserved, they thought, their pity, and even indignation, and his request was such as became a man to ask and men to grant; they gave him permission to enrol his son in the register of his fraternity, giving him his own name. This son afterward, after having defeated the Peloponnesians at Arginusae, was, with his fellow-generals, put to death by the people.

(38) About the time when his son was enrolled, it should seem the plague seized Pericles, not with sharp and violent fits, as it did others that had it, but with a dull and lingering distemper, attended with various changes and alterations, leisurely, by little and little, wasting the strength of his body, and undermining the noble faculties of his soul. So that Theophrastus, in his *Morals,* when discussing whether men's characters change with their circumstances, and their moral habits,

disturbed by the ailings of their bodies, start aside from the rules of virtue, has left it upon record, that Pericles, when he was sick, showed one of his friends that came to visit him an amulet or charm that the women had hung about his neck; as much as to say, that he was very sick indeed when he would admit of such a foolery as that was.

When he was now near his end, the best of the citizens and those of his friends who were left alive, sitting about him, were speaking of the greatness of his merit, and his power, and reckoning up his famous actions and the number of his victories; for there were no less than nine trophies, which, as their chief commander and conqueror of their enemies, he had set up for the honour of the city. They talked thus together among themselves, as though he were unable to understand or mind what they said, but had now lost his consciousness. He had listened, however, all the while, and attended to all, and, speaking out among them, said that he wondered they should commend and take notice of things which were as much owing to fortune as to anything else, and had happened to many other commanders, and, at the same time, should not speak or make mention of that which was the most excellent and greatest thing of all. "For," said he, "no Athenian, through my means, ever wore mourning."

(39) He was indeed a character deserving our high admiration not only for his equitable and mild temper, which all along in the many affairs of his life, and the great animosities which he incurred, he constantly maintained; but also for the high spirit and feeling which made him regard it, the noblest of all his honours that, in the exercise of such immense power, he never had gratified his envy or his passion, nor ever had treated any enemy as irreconcilably opposed to him. And to me it appears that this one thing gives that otherwise childish and arrogant title a fitting and becoming significance; so dispassionate a temper, a life so pure and unblemished, in the height of power and place, might well be called Olympian, in accordance with our conceptions of the divine beings, to whom, as the natural authors of all good and of nothing evil, we ascribe the rule and government of the world. Not as the poets represent, who, while confounding us with their ignorant

fancies, are themselves confuted by their own poems and fictions, and call the place, indeed, where they say the gods make their abode, a secure and quiet seat, free from all hazards and commotions, untroubled with winds or with clouds, and equally through all time illumined with a soft serenity and a pure light as though such were a home most agreeable for a blessed and immortal nature; and yet, in the meanwhile, affirm that the gods themselves are full of trouble and enmity and anger and other passions, which no way become or belong to even men that have any understanding. But this will, perhaps seem a subject fitter for some other consideration, and that ought to be treated of in some other place.

The course of public affairs after his death produced a quick and speedy sense of the loss of Pericles. Those who, while he lived, resented his great authority, as that which eclipsed themselves, presently after his quitting the stage, making trial of other orators and demagogues, readily acknowledged that there never had been in nature such a disposition as his was, more moderate and reasonable in the height of that state he took upon him, or more grave and impressive in the mildness which he used. And that invidious arbitrary power, to which formerly they gave the name of monarchy and tyranny, did then appear to have been the chief bulwark of public safety; so great a corruption and such a flood of mischief and vice followed which he, by keeping weak and low, had withheld from notice, and had prevented from attaining incurable height through a licentious impunity.

RECOMMENDED READING

The following books or articles can be commended to supplement the student's reading.

ON PERICLES

Ehrenberg, V. *Sophocles and Pericles.* Oxford, 1954.

Kagan, D. *Pericles of Athens and the Birth of Democracy.* New York, 1991.

Podlecki, A. *Perikles and His Circle.* London, 1998. This is an approachable, yet detailed and scholarly, account.

Samons, L., II, ed. *The Cambridge Companion to the Age of Pericles.* Cambridge, 2007.

ON ASPASIA

Henry, M. *Prisoner of History: Aspasia of Miletus and Her Biographical Tradition.* Oxford, 1995.

ON THE PLAGUE

Holladay, A. J., and J. C. F. Poole. "Thucydides and the Plague of Athens." *Classical Quarterly* 29 (1979): 282–300.
Morgan, T. E. "Plague or Poetry? Thucydides on the Epidemic at Athens." *Transactions of the American Philological Association* 124 (1994): 197–208.

ON THUCYDIDES

Dover, K. J. *Thucydides.* Greece and Rome New Surveys in the Classics 7. Oxford, 1973.
Finley, J. H. *Thucydides.* Cambridge, Mass., 1942. Despite its age, still one of the best books on Thucydides.
Hornblower, S. *Thucydides.* Baltimore, 1987.
Rawlings, H. *The Structure of Thucydides' History.* Princeton, 1981.
Strassler, R. B. *The Landmark Thucydides.* New York, 1996. A revised edition of the Richard Crawley translation with excellent maps.
Thucydides. *The Peloponnesian War.* Translated with introduction and notes by Steven Lattimore. Indianapolis, 1999. A good translation of the complete history.

ON THE ATHENIAN EMPIRE

Meiggs, R. *The Athenian Empire.* Oxford, 1982. A full and scholarly treatment.
Rhodes, P. J. *The Athenian Empire.* Greece and Rome New Surveys in the Classics 17. Oxford, 1985.

ON THE ATHENIAN ACROPOLIS

Hurwit, J. M. *The Athenian Acropolis.* Cambridge, 2001.

GLOSSARY

ABDERA. Coastal city of Thrace in northern Greece (map 2), birthplace of Protagoras.

ACARNANIA. Region of northwest Greece on the Ionian Sea (map 1). It was strategically located on the sailing route west to Italy and played an important role in the power struggles of the fifth century between Athens and Sparta and their allies.

ACHARNAE. Largest deme or subdivision of Attica, about 7 1/2 miles north of Athens (map 4). It lay in the path of the Spartan advance into Attica in 431.

ACROPOLIS. Word meaning "high city" and designating the fortified citadel of a Greek city. The Acropolis at Athens (fig. 4) contained a number of the most important religious shrines of the Athenians. The Parthenon was located here, and here the Athenians kept the treasury of the empire.

AEGINA. Island in the Saronic Gulf opposite Athens' main harbor at Piraeus (map 4). It was forced to become part of Athens' naval empire in 458/7. Aeginetan complaints to the Spartans about Athenian treatment contributed to the start of the

Peloponnesian War and led to a complete Athenian takeover
of the island in 431, shortly after the war began.

AEGOSPOTAMI. Small town and river on the European side of the
Hellespont in the Thracian Chersonese, north and east of
Sestos (map 2), where the Athenian fleet suffered its final
defeat at the hands of the Spartans in 405.

AGARISTE. Mother of Pericles and niece of Cleisthenes of Athens
(fig. 8), the founder of Athenian democracy.

ALCIBIADES. Ward of Pericles, follower of Socrates, and controversial
general and politician (451/0–404/3).

ALCMAEONIDS. Prominent and noble Athenian family to which
Pericles and Alcibiades belonged on their mothers' sides.
Cleisthenes and Megacles were also members of this family
(fig. 8).

AMPHIPOLIS. Main city in southern Thrace, located just north of the
Chalcidic Peninsula (map 2). It was colonized in 437/6 by the
Athenians and owed its importance to its strategic position on
the trade routes. In 424 it surrendered to the Spartans.

ANAXAGORAS. Ionian philosopher (ca. 500–ca. 428) from Clazomenae
in Asia Minor (map 2) who was interested in the physical
nature of the universe. He was probably an associate of Pericles
and may have been attacked in the law courts on that account.

ARCHIDAMUS. Spartan king who ruled for over forty years. He was a
friend of Pericles and king at the start of the Peloponnesian
War. As king he led the first invasions of Attica. He died
in 427.

ARCHON. Title for the nine traditional leading officials of the Athenian
state. A person could serve only once as archon, and the term of
office was one year. The first chosen gave his name to the year;
thus the Athenians dated events by this archon's name: "When
so and so was archon, such and such happened." After 487/6
they were chosen by lot. After stepping down from office they
automatically became members of the Council of the
Areopagus.

AREOPAGUS. Rocky outcropping on the northwest slope of the
Acropolis. The council of ex-archons, known as the Council of
the Areopagus (see below), met here.

ARGINOUSAE. Small islands off the coast of Asia Minor near Lesbos
(map 2) where the Athenian fleet won a victory over the
Spartans in 406. Unfortunately a storm developed and
prevented the commanders from recovering survivors. Pericles
the Younger was among the commanders condemned and
executed for that failure.

ARGOS. Major city in the southern part of the Argive Plain (maps 1
and 5) with a very long history. The Argives were on-again,
off-again allies of Corinth and the Spartans. In the "First
Peloponnesian War" in 461 and again in 420 they made an
alliance with the Athenians against the Spartans.

ARISTEIDES. Athenian general and statesman, known as "the Just." He
led troops at the battle of Salamis and was one of the main
commanders at the rout of the Persians at Plataea in 479. He
helped form the Delian League and was responsible for levying
the first contributions of the allies.

BOEOTIA. Major geographical region of Greece, located to the north
and west of Attica (map 1). Its capital was Thebes (map 4). The
Boeotians and Athenians shared a common boundary and were
traditional enemies, similar to France and Germany in modern
Europe.

BRASIDAS. Energetic Spartan commander who won many successes in
the first decade of the Peloponnesian War, first in the
Peloponnese and later in Thrace. He kept the historian and
general Thucydides from holding Amphipolis (map 2) and, by
doing so, caused his exile. Brasidas died of wounds fighting in
the north in 422.

CADMUS. Founder and first king of Thebes in Boeotia (map 4).

CALLIAS. Young follower of Socrates and kinsman of Pericles who was
notorious in his youth for his wealth and extravagant lifestyle.
Born about 450, he lived until 370 and served as general in

391/0. He figures in Xenophon's *Symposium* and Plato's *Protagoras*.

CERAMICUS. Potters' quarter of Athens, located to the northwest of the main market square, just outside the main gate of the city. One of the most important cemeteries of the ancient city was located here. It was the site of public burials of the war dead and Pericles' funeral oration.

CHAERONEIA. City in north Boeotia (map 1), birthplace of Plutarch.

CHOLARGUS. Deme or subdivision of Attica about 4 miles as the crow flies north and slightly west of the Acropolis in the foothills of Mount Aegaleos (map 4). Pericles' family hailed from this deme, and their estates were located here.

CIMON. Son of Miltiades who frequently served as general and commanded many operations of the Delian League. A political opponent of Pericles, he was unsuccessfully prosecuted by Pericles for accepting bribes in 463, and was ostracized in 461. He returned from exile at the end of the 450s and died fighting for Athens against the Persians on Cyprus about 450.

CLEISTHENES. Athenian politician and reformer of the Alcmaeonid family (fig. 8) and archon in 525/4. He carried out a reorganization of the citizen body of Athens in 506, creating the demes and tribes that served as the basis for participation in the political life of the city. He is often regarded as the founder of Athenian democracy.

CLEON. Leader in Athens after Pericles' death. He was general at Pylos (map 1) in 425, when the Athenians defeated the Spartans, and was killed in battle outside Amphipolis (map 2) in 422. An effective speaker who could sway the populace, he appears to have had no compunctions about appealing to the baser instincts of the people.

CORINTH. Major city located on the isthmus connecting northern Greece and the Peloponnese (maps 1 and 5). Its leaders opposed Athens actively and were instrumental in persuading the Spartans to declare war.

COUNCIL OF THE AREOPAGUS. Council composed of men who had served as archons, thus constituting an advisory group of elder statesmen. This group was fairly conservative and a power base for the aristocrats. In the emergency of the Persian invasion of 480–479 it came to play a major role in policy making. Ephialtes successfully removed most of these powers in 462/1 and reduced the Council of the Areopagus to a law court that presided over homicide cases involving Athenian citizens.

CRATINUS. One of the greatest writers of Old Comedy, active from the 440s to the 420s. We know of twenty-seven titles by Cratinus and have about five hundred citations of his work.

CYRUS THE YOUNGER. Prince of the Persian empire who about 408 joined in an alliance with the Spartans against the Athenians and led his army against them in Asia Minor. According to Thucydides, he provided money to the Spartans to build a fleet.

DARIUS. King of Persia and father of Xerxes. His army was defeated by the Athenians at Marathon (maps 1, 2, and 4) in 490.

DELIAN LEAGUE. Defensive alliance formed by the Athenians and their allies in 478/7 to keep the Persians out of the Aegean Sea (map 2). The League eventually became the Athenian naval empire.

DEMOSTHENES. Athenian general whose actions at Pylos (map 1) led to the capture of a large number of Spartan soldiers in 425. He was sent to Sicily in 413 with reinforcements for the Athenian forces, commanded the rear guard in the futile overland retreat from Syracuse, and was captured and executed.

ELEUSIS. Well-known deme or subdivision of Attica located northwest of Athens on a sheltered bay in the fertile Thriasian Plain (map 4). The town was famous for the celebration of the mysteries in honor of the goddess of grain and fertility, Demeter, and her daughter Kore.

EPHIALTES. Little-known Athenian politician. Supported by Pericles, he passed measures about 462 that deprived the aristocratic Council of the Areopagus of political power. Not long afterward he was assassinated.

EPIDAMNUS. Colony of Corcyra (Corfu) and Corinth on the Adriatic coast (map 2). Fighting over the colony between the Corcyraeans and the Corinthians led to the start of the Peloponnesian War.

EPIDAURUS. Small city-state on the coast of the northeast Peloponnese across the Saronic Gulf from Athens (map 5). It was an ally of Sparta in the Peloponnesian War.

EUBOEA. Long, narrow island located off the coasts of Boeotia and Attica to the northeast (map 1). Its chief cities were Chalcis and Eretria. It came under control of Athens in the late sixth century and revolted in 446. Pericles brought it back under Athenian influence.

EUPOLIS. One of the great poets of Athenian Old Comedy who produced his first play in 429 and died sometime after 415 in the region of the Hellespont. We have the titles of nineteen plays and almost five hundred citations from his work. In his *Demes,* produced about 417, he summoned great Athenians of the past from the underworld to advise the city, among whom was Pericles.

GORGIAS. Influential teacher of rhetoric from the city of Leontini in Sicily who came to Athens in 427 and exercised great influence there. Plato named his *Gorgias* for him and makes him a featured speaker in it. Isocrates was one of his students.

GREAT KING. Title referring to the king of the Persians, who was also styled King of Kings.

HADRIAN. Emperor of Rome and philhellene who ruled from A.D. 117 to 138.

HAGNON. Founder of Amphipolis (map 2) in 437/6 and a general in the opening years of the Peloponnesian War.

HALICARNASSUS. City on the coast of southern Asia Minor, birthplace of the historian Herodotus (map 2).

HALIEIS. Small coastal town south of Troizen in the Argolid/northeast Peloponnese that was occupied by the Athenians during the Peloponnesian War (map 5).

HERM. Stone pillar with a head on top and a phallus, sacred to the god Hermes, especially in Athens. The mutilation of herms one night in 415 was a notable scandal involving Critias and perhaps Alcibiades. In later times, portrait busts of well-known men were often represented on herms.

HERMES. Major Olympian god who was a messenger and skilled in trickery and deception. One of his main functions was to guide the souls of the dead to the underworld. He is often represented as a stone pillar with a head on top and a phallus. *See* herm.

HERMIONE. Coastal town in the northeast Peloponnese south of Troizen and north of Halieis (map 5). An ally of Sparta, it was plundered by the Athenians in 430.

ION OF CHIOS. Versatile writer who wrote tragedies and satyr plays as well as prose works. Later critics considered him one of the five greatest tragedians, but none of his plays is extant. Born about 480, he came to Athens about 465. Reference is made to an account he wrote of a visit he had with Pericles.

ISAGORAS. Obscurely known Athenian politician of the late sixth century who tried with the support of the Spartans to oppose Cleisthenes.

ISOCRATES. Athenian orator who studied with Socrates as a young man. He did not come into prominence until the fourth century, when he became a teacher of rhetoric. Born in 436, he lived to be almost 100, dying in 338.

LACEDAEMON. Name frequently used by Thucydides for Sparta and its territory.

LACONIA. Name of the eastern half of the southern Peloponnese (map 5), where the city of Sparta was located.

LYCURGUS. Athenian politician (ca. 390–325) who came to prominence after 338. He restored Athens financially and looked to Pericles as a model.

MARATHON. Deme or subdivision of Attica on its northeast coast (maps 1, 2 and 4) and site of the famous battle in 490 in which the citizen army of Athens routed the Persians.

MEDES. Old-fashioned word for Persians. A person charged with Medism was considered a traitor, a Persian sympathizer.

MEGARA. City between Athens and Corinth, and sometime ally of the Spartans (maps 1 and 5).

METIC. Foreigner who came to Athens and chose to become a permanent resident. A metic was subject to a tax and to military service.

MILETUS. One of the great cities on the southern coast of Asia Minor (map 2), a major sea power, and home of several famous early philosophers, namely, Thales, Anaximander, and Anaximenes. Pericles' Aspasia also was a Milesian by birth.

MILTIADES. Father of Cimon and one of the generals who led the Athenians in their victory over the Persians at the battle of Marathon (maps 1, 2, and 4) in 490.

MUNYCHIA. Fortified hill in the port of Piraeus (see map 3).

MYTILENE. Major city of the island of Lesbos in the eastern Aegean (map 2). An ally of Athens, it revolted in 428. The Athenians put down the revolt and, in a famous debate recorded by Thucydides (3.36 ff.), first decided to execute all the males of the city, but then reversed their decision the next day.

NICIAS. Wealthy Athenian general (ca. 470–413) and one of the leaders of the city after the death of Pericles. He sought peace with Sparta, and the truce of 421 bears his name. He later served as general in the disastrous campaign against Sicily and was executed there.

OEDIPUS. Mythical king of Thebes in Boeotia (map 4) who killed his father and married his mother. When he found out what he had done, he blinded himself. Sophocles tells his story in the tragedy *Oedipus the King*.

OENOE. Small, fortified Athenian garrison town guarding the pass into Attica from Boeotia (map 4). It was the first place attacked by King Archidamus and his troops when the Peloponnesian War began in 431.

PARALUS. Son of Pericles, named after an Athenian hero of the same name who was the patron of sailors. He was about thirty years old when he died of the plague around the beginning of the Peloponnesian War. Almost nothing else is known about him.

PAUSANIAS. Spartan king and commander of the combined Greek forces at the battle of Plataea (map 1) in 479. He later died in disgrace.

PEISISTRATUS. Benevolent tyrant of Athens who seized power about 560 and ruled with his sons until his death in 527. Athens was prosperous under his rule, and he was probably responsible for building projects on the Acropolis and for the enhancement of the festivals of the city.

PELOPONNESE. Literally the island of Pelops, legendary king of the area around Olympia in southern Greece (see map 1). Thucydides uses the term Peloponnese to refer to the whole of southern Greece and the term Peloponnesians to refer to the Spartans and their allies.

PHALERON. First harbor of the city of Athens, directly east of Piraeus harbor (map 3). It remained important as part of the naval complex and was protected by the fortification walls connecting the city with the port.

PHIDIAS. Athenian sculptor and associate of Pericles who was probably in charge of the entire program of sculptural decoration for the Parthenon (fig. 5). His most famous creations were the gold-and-ivory statues of Athena in the Parthenon and Zeus at Olympia. His Athena was installed in 438. Shortly after this, Phidias was attacked in the courts and left Athens to work at Olympia.

PLEISTOANAX. Spartan king whom Pericles is rumored to have bribed to withdraw from Attica (map 1) when he invaded in 446.

POTIDAEA. Colony of Corinth on the Chalcidic Peninsula (map 2), but also a member of the Delian League. Athens imposed a heavy levy on it in 434, and, when it revolted in the year 432, the Athenians laid siege and eventually took it over.

PROPYLAEA. Grand covered entryway (fig. 6) to the Athenian
Acropolis (figs. 4 and 7) designed by the architect Mnesicles
and constructed in 437–432. The Peloponnesian War
interrupted work on it, and it was never completely finished.

SAMOS. Large Aegean island next to the coast of Asia Minor just north
of Miletus (map 2). It possessed a powerful navy and was an
ally of the Athenians in the Delian League. When it revolted in
440, Pericles and Sophocles were active as generals in putting
down the revolt.

SICILIAN EXPEDITION. Great expedition sent out by the Athenians in
415 to take control of Sicily and ending in disastrous defeat in
413 with the loss of many men and ships.

SICYON. City-state located on the fertile coastal plain west of Corinth
(map 1). Cleisthenes, an early ruler (ca. 585), held a famous
contest for the hand of his daughter Agariste. She was won by
Megacles, a noble Athenian of the Alcmaeonid family (fig. 8).
During the Peloponnesian War, Sicyon was an ally of Corinth
and Sparta.

SOLON. Athenian politician, lawgiver, and poet. As archon in 594/3, he
gave, it appears, more power to the poorer classes and
strengthened the assembly and the judicial system.

SPHINX. Hybrid creature with a human head and the body of an
animal, usually a lion, and often winged. The Sphinx of the
Oedipus tale waylaid passersby and killed those who failed to
solve her riddle.

STESIMBROTUS OF THASOS. Teacher of the late fifth century who
lectured at Athens and wrote on Homer and Homeric
interpretation. He also wrote sketches of Athenian political
leaders, including Themistocles and Pericles, which contained
scurrilous details. His purpose is uncertain, but he appears to
have been contemptuous of the democracy and its leaders.

TALENT. Weight standard used for currency in the ancient world. One
talent equaled 6,000 Attic drachmas or a weight of almost 57
pounds.

TELECLEIDES. Athenian poet of Old Comedy who was active in the 440s.

THEBES. Capital of Boeotia and site of the Oedipus story (map 4).

THEMISTOCLES. Athenian statesman and general (ca. 524–ca. 459) who developed Athenian sea power and was the architect of the naval victory over the Persians at Salamis (maps 1 and 4) in 480.

THRACIAN CHERSONESE. Spit of land that forms the western side of the Hellespont (map 2), location of Sestos.

THRIASIAN PLAIN. Fertile land around Eleusis (map 4).

THUCYDIDES SON OF MELESIAS. Athenian politician (to be distinguished from the historian Thucydides, to whom he may have been related). He was related to Cimon, succeeded Cimon as the leading rival of Pericles, and was ostracized in 443.

THURII. Greek colony founded in 444/3 on the site of Sybaris in southern Italy by the Athenians and other Greeks together with citizens of the former Sybaris (map 2). The historian Herodotus settled there toward the end of his life, and Protagoras, it was said, wrote its first law code at Pericles' invitation. The speechwriter Lysias also lived there for some years.

TOLMIDES. Athenian general and contemporary of Pericles who led an expedition into Boeotia (maps 1 and 4) in 447 and was defeated by a combined force of Boeotians at the town of Coronea. He perished in the battle.

TRAJAN. Emperor of Rome from A.D. 98 to 117.

TROIZEN. City-state southeast of Corinth on the northeast coast of the Peloponnese (map 5). A Spartan ally, it was attacked on several occasions during the Peloponnesian War.

XANTHIPPUS. (1) Pericles' father, a prominent politician ostracized in 484 and successful general in the Persian Wars; (2) the older of Pericles' legitimate sons, who was about thirty-five when he died of the plague in the summer of 430 (fig. 8).

XERXES. King of the Persian empire from 486 to 465 B.C. and leader of the great invasion of Greece that led to the battles at Salamis (480) and Plataea (479) (map 1), where his forces were defeated.

INDEX